LETTING
GO OF YOUR
LIMITATIONS

Page 13, 12, 14, 19,

LETTING
GO OF YOUR
LIMITATIONS

*Experiencing God's
Transforming Power*

SANDIE FREED

Chosen

a division of Baker Publishing Group
Minneapolis, Minnesota

© 2013 by Sandie Freed

Published by Chosen Books
11400 Hampshire Avenue South
Bloomington, Minnesota 55438
www.chosenbooks.com

Chosen Books is a division of
Baker Publishing Group, Grand Rapids, Michigan

Printed in the United States of America

Library of Congress Cataloging-in-Publication Data is on file at the Library of Congress, Washington, DC.

ISBN 978-0-8007-9563-4 (pbk.)

Unless otherwise indicated, Scripture taken from the HOLY BIBLE, NEW INTERNATIONAL VERSION®. Copyright © 1973, 1978, 1984 Biblica. Used by permission of Zondervan. All rights reserved.

Scripture quotations identified AMPLIFIED are from the Amplified® Bible, copyright © 1954, 1958, 1962, 1964, 1965, 1987 by The Lockman Foundation. Used by permission.

Scripture quotations identified NASB are from the New American Standard Bible®, copyright © 1960, 1962, 1963, 1968, 1971, 1972, 1973, 1975, 1977, 1995 by The Lockman Foundation. Used by permission.

Scripture quotations identified NKJV are from the New King James Version. Copyright © 1982 by Thomas Nelson, Inc. Used by permission. All rights reserved.

Scripture quotations identified NLT are from the *Holy Bible*, New Living Translation, copyright © 1996, 2004, 2007 by Tyndale House Foundation. Used by permission of Tyndale House Publishers, Inc., Carol Stream, Illinois 60188. All rights reserved.

Scripture quotations identified KJV are from the King James Version of the Bible.

Cover design by DogEared Design

13   14   15   16   17   18   19   7   6   5   4   3   2   1

Contents

Acknowledgments

Over the years many people have asked me how I get time to write—especially since I have written more than eleven books in close to nine years. It's not so much the *time* for me as much as the *village* required to keep me moving in a positive and productive direction!

With that in mind, I could never list all the fellow villagers who are on this pilgrimage with me as we truly seek Kingdom revelation that is both needed and yet still timely. However, I lovingly dedicate this book to . . .

Jesus Christ

. . . the One who sacrificed His life so that I might be righteous. He removed my need to be perfect, do everything right and measure up to what *I* think is necessary to please Him. I now know that I am righteous *only* because of what was accomplished at the cross.

Mickey, my husband

. . . the man God gave me. You have seen the good, the

bad and the ugly, and you have remained my helpmate for over forty years. Thank you for always believing in me.

My family

. . . especially my sister, Pam Garris, who has always been the wind beneath my wings. Thank you for all of your love and support over the years. To my daughter, Kimberly, I love you. You are still the best thing I ever did.

My church family

. . . to my spiritual oversight, Bishop and Evelyn Hamon, thank you for being a mom and dad whenever no one else believed I could be used for God's glory. You saw something in me that I could not see. Thank you for your prophetic vision and your divine direction over the last several decades! And, dear Bishop, thank you additionally for theologically reviewing all my books and writing the forewords for most of them (I know how busy you are!). Your prophetic wisdom and insight have been priceless to me over the years.

. . . to Jim and Jeannie Davis, my friends and co-laborers. I want to thank you for being loyal and committed friends for over 25 years. And, Dr. Jim, thank you for theologically reviewing all of my articles, studies and books. You both have been instrumental in introducing me to God's grace and divine love.

. . . to Zion Ministries and Lifegate Church International, thank you for all your intercession, prayers and loyal commitments. To our new (and very anointed) assistant pastors and worship leaders, Bob and Cindy Guidry, I thank you so much for coming on board and remaining dedicated to promoting God's Kingdom.

. . . to our leaders and intercessors, I could not have done this again without your support! You pray and believe, and therefore we witness divine results! Thank you. Words could never express my admiration and appreciation for all of you.

. . . and a very special thank-you to Paula Bledsoe, who does all of the original personal editing (and is my personal assistant). Endless hours have been spent editing and re-editing, organizing and re-organizing, scheduling and re-scheduling . . . and tracking my airline flights.

. . . to my Chosen Books family. Goodness, how could I come up with enough words to thank my family at Chosen Books? I am so thrilled, honored and humbled to work with one of the best editorial directors ever—Jane Campbell! Oh my goodness, what a gift she is to the Body of Christ. And a special thanks to Ann Weinheimer, my personal editor who worked with me to perfect this book before print—thank you! I love you and how you make me look good on paper! You are such a gift to me. Still, there is so much more to this Chosen Books team and their various departments that are too long to list—but you know who you are. Thank you so much for including me in your family!

We are doing His divine will together to establish His Kingdom on earth!

Introduction

God's plans for His servants follow many avenues. Some avenues seem to resemble previous ones traveled; others challenge us with new twists and turns. Yet as we journey with *purpose,* we are fulfilling destiny—all to bring glory to God.

The word *purpose* means "the reason something exists." Mankind as a whole was created in the image of God with the purpose of multiplying and subduing (taking dominion over) the earth. God also created each of us individually for a specific purpose, and we exist to fulfill that purpose.

Our greatest purpose, of course, is to *give God glory*. In fact, He desires to "show us off." But He also desires for us to show Him off to the world. God is a good God—this book will always point in that direction. God *is* love; love cannot be separated from Him.

As we journey together, we will explore the power of God and learn how to experience it today. We will become more aware of what it means to follow in the footsteps of

Jesus, who was victorious in His original purpose: "For this purpose the Son of God was manifested, that He might destroy the works of the devil" (1 John 3:8 KJV).

The Greek translation of *purpose* reveals that it is connected to the word *tupos* (pronounced *too*-pos) meaning "model or imitation." This shows us clearly that Jesus, who destroyed all the works of the devil, came as a model for us to imitate. I am not a person who uses my magnifying glass to search for demons under every bush, but when the Lord reveals hidden mysteries with the intent to set captives free and imbue us with His power, I am on it!

Yet even as we embrace our purpose and the loving plans of our Father for our lives, too often it seems that we are held back, bound by limitations in our own hearts and minds. We believe that God's transforming power is available, but we cannot grasp it. The Church today is often little help, for she has become anemic in demonstrating the Kingdom of God on earth.

This is nothing new. The apostle Paul spoke to this situation after his ministry on Mars Hill, where he confronted a city that prided itself on its mental prowess. The Greeks took pride in their knowledge, and the work of the enemy today is leading Christians to follow this same path.

That is why I have chosen to begin our study—the first few chapters—by using the life of Paul as a framework for breaking free from our limitations. Paul, once the brilliant persecutor of Christians, was transformed into the Church's foremost missionary of the Gospel. He taught how legalism and intellectualism, particularly as they are based in pride, rob the Church and limit her effectiveness against evil. Then we will look at the disciples' failure to grasp a powerful message because their minds were not renewed. We will explore Jeremiah's call—and the power of our words.

It is my heart's desire to experience God's supernatural, transforming power in my life today, and I am certain that you feel the same. In this book, therefore, I examine many limitations that keep us from enjoying the freedom that Christ died to give us. In order to let go of these limitations—some self-imposed, some pressed upon us—we will battle many spirits: legalism, intellectualism, Pharisaism, judgmentalism, religion, self-righteousness, guilt, shame. All of these dangers are easily identifiable in the lives of those God has transformed, as we will see in many scriptural examples. It is a question of purpose. Any life goal we try to achieve apart from the saving grace of Jesus will end in death—no matter how noble it may sound. Only the resurrection power of Jesus can change us into His likeness. Out of death and into life.

As we explore together, we will take a deep look into our hearts and examine our motives. We will ask ourselves such questions as:

- Am I experiencing the power of God in my life?
- Am I qualified to demonstrate God's power?
- Am I struggling with shame and guilt, and do I, therefore, believe I am not worthy of God's using me and mantling me with His power?
- Do I *really* believe God is good and that He loves me?
- Am I serving God out of duty or out of love?
- Do I want a relationship with God or with religion?
- Am I more comfortable following written rules and regulations than trusting in my relationship with God?

- Am I so intellectual that I hinder the power of God from manifesting in me and through me?
- Am I serving God while seeking my own glory and self-fulfillment?
- Do I fully understand what resurrection power is?
- Am I expecting God to resurrect my dreams, my success and my heart's desires?
- Am I believing that God has given me the means to have wealth through His resurrection power?

You see, dear believer, God does not want you to be limited in fulfilling your purpose. *Sozo* is the Greek word for *salvation*. But this word means so much more than being "saved." It means so much more than simply getting "fire insurance." *Sozo* means being "saved, healed, delivered, protected, restored." God wants to give us the full inheritance we have through Christ Jesus. This book is designed to help explain that inheritance. As you continue to read, you will gain understanding about your authority and your ability to experience God's transforming power—both in you personally and in the world around you—because of your seated position in Christ Jesus.

For too long, much of the Church has backed away from opposition by the devil. We will have to stand our ground to experience the power of God. Choosing the path of least resistance will never promote the Kingdom of God. In fact, we can expect opposition when we have made up our minds to follow Christ and promote His Kingdom on earth.

Believer, we must *all* be careful not to judge, condemn or hold tightly to personal doctrines when Christ is *always* exposing truth. Are we listening to the voice of the Holy

Spirit—especially when mysteries are being revealed in this present day?

Let's turn our attention to the first chapter, which gives us an overview of how the spirit of legalism sets itself against God's anointed. As you begin reading, I encourage you to ask yourself if you are daily opening your heart to the voice of the Holy Spirit. Like Paul, any one of us at any time can be a persecutor of Christ and truth if our religion and doctrines have become our "sacred cows." Let us daily ask Him to open the eyes of our hearts and minds so that we may truly see Him as He is. As He removes the veils from our eyes, He also will empower us with an understanding of Kingdom living.

My prayer for you as we journey together in this book is based upon Paul's prayer for the Ephesian church:

> Dear ones, I will continue to thank the Lord for you and remember you in my prayers. I pray that the God of our Lord Jesus Christ will give you a spirit of wisdom and revelation so that you will grow in your relationship with Him. I pray also that the eyes of your heart will be full of light and truth and that the Word of God would become illuminated within you so that you walk in the power and demonstration of the Spirit of God. I also pray that you will have full understanding and knowledge of the hope to which He has called you and that you will witness and experience the glorious inheritance He has provided for His set-apart ones—which includes you! Amen.
>
> Ephesians 1:16–19 (paraphrased)

Now, precious believer, join me in finding freedom from every limitation that keeps us from receiving Jesus' grace and the power of His might. He is mantling you with power right now. As you examine your heart and your mind, you will receive renewed strength each day to fulfill your purpose in Christ—and experience His transforming power.

1

The Persecutor

Letting Go of "Religion"

S tone him! Stone him!

    As Stephen was seized and dragged toward the city gates of Jerusalem, Saul nodded his support of the angry, shouting crowd. Stephen, a young apostle of that one who had claimed to be the Messiah, was an enemy of *true religion*—Saul was convinced of this—and in his heart he wanted Stephen dead.

    Saul stepped back as the angry men swept past him. Yet the force of the mob, as it pushed Stephen along, shoved Saul into a doorway. "Hey, watch it!" Saul yelled. But as he got a closer look at the accused, Saul shook his head. *Amazing. I have seen him study with my mentor, Gamaliel. How could this happen? Gamaliel is a devoted and astute teacher. How could Stephen forsake his teaching—all he has learned under the tutelage of Judaism—and follow a false prophet?*

Saul was born in Tarsus and was, therefore, a Roman citizen. Having received his Jewish teaching in Jerusalem, Saul was in the city that day to worship in the synagogue and to meet with Gamaliel, an esteemed Pharisee who had intense appreciation for Greek culture. Gamaliel's leadership had contributed significantly to Saul's lofty intellectualism and his character in general.

Saul thought about Stephen, who seemed so young. Saul himself was close to thirty years of age. He continued to watch the crowd, many of whom began to pick up stones and grip them tightly. Saul grabbed a few as well, mainly to empower others in their anger and hatred.

Though stoning was gruesome, Saul was pleased with the sentencing. His position within the Sanhedrin—and his knowledge of the Law with its strict judgments of those who opposed it—made Saul even more proud of being on the right side of this execution. *Yes,* he thought, *anyone who forsakes the Law deserves to be punished—and even executed.*

"Here!" One man in the crowd yelled and signaled others over toward Saul. "Everyone leave your coats here and gather your stones."

Men began removing their outer garments and slinging them at the feet of Saul. They could not disrobe fast enough, for religious zeal can transform quickly into violent hatred. Saul thought to himself, *Stoning someone to death is dirty work; yet one need not tear his robe or dirty himself—or bloody himself—in the act. And arms must be free of any encumbrances so that stones can be hurled at full strength.*

Saul sighed. *I have other important matters to attend to, but I'll watch anyway. I owe it to the other members of the Sanhedrim to stay and bear witness. And I really should make sure that the garments are properly returned to the executors.* Saul kept his vigil.

The Ease of Deception

While this account of Saul witnessing the stoning of Stephen comes from my imagination, it is biblically based. In Acts 6–8 the story of Stephen is outlined, and Saul's support is irrefutable. In fact, the first verse of Acts 8 says: "Saul was there, giving approval to [Stephen's] death."

We first learn of Saul through this story of Stephen, and Saul's attitude is shocking. In fact, it is almost barbaric. His hatred for those with religious differences erased any compassion or tolerance for human life he might otherwise have had. So what made the change in him? God broke through the many limitations darkening his heart and mind.

I believe that a study of the life of Saul—we will look closely at his experiences in the first four chapters of this book—opens the door to greater revelation of how we ourselves limit the demonstration and power of God from flowing freely in our lives. We encounter spirits of legalism, intellectualism, Pharisaism, judgmentalism, religion, self-righteousness, guilt and shame every day—as did Saul. And like Saul, we run the risk of allowing these spirits and all their counterparts to drive us. Saul believed that he was *right* in his religion, and until Jesus met him on the Damascus Road nothing was going to deter him.

19

Do you see the parallels today? Satan has not laid aside this very effective means of deceiving people. Judgment? Self-righteousness? Even Pharisaism? These are prevalent in the Church. Believers are being blocked in our Kingdom work because we are not experiencing God's transforming power—both within our lives and through our lives to the world around us.

It is so easy to be convinced that *our way* is always the *right way*, or that our belief systems are always the right belief systems. Stephen's teaching did not line up with the teaching of the Sanhedrin, and Saul would not put up with it. While the Bible does not say that Saul threw a single stone at Stephen, he was just as guilty as those who did because he gave consent. He committed murder in his heart.

Let's back up to the beginning of Acts 7 to gain greater understanding of just what it was that provoked the Pharisees to commit murder.

Stephen's Accusers: The Religious System

We are told in Acts 6 and 7 that Stephen's religious opponents, who belonged to a fellowship of Jewish men called the Synagogue of the Freedmen, disputed with Stephen but could not refute "the wisdom and the Spirit" by which Stephen spoke (Acts 6:10 NKJV). Driven by jealousy, they secretly induced false witnesses to accuse him of blasphemy, a crime punishable by death. The people became so stirred up by this, they brought him before the Sanhedrin for judgment.

Stephen had been preaching the Gospel of Christ, and his preaching had been adding converts, including priests, to the Church daily. In addition, Stephen had been working mighty miracles among the people. Indeed, he was turning the city upside down!

But Stephen's preaching and actions threatened the Sanhedrin and their religious system. After all, they believed that their *knowledge* of God and their *works* for God guaranteed their right relationship with God.

During his trial, Stephen did not back down from his calling. Because the Church was growing so fast and had many needs, he, along with six others, had been chosen by the Twelve to oversee distribution of food among those in need. Each of them was chosen because he was "full of the Holy Spirit and wisdom" (Acts 6:3 NKJV). Stephen had been showing what a life that experiences the transforming power of God can do. He did not teach religion; he demonstrated the heart of God. It was because this threatened their religious order that Stephen was dragged before the Sanhedrin.

The crowd grew quiet. All eyes were on the young man. The high priest remained seated as he listened to the "witnesses," then he turned to Stephen. "Are these charges true?" he asked.

Stephen answered with a message from heaven, which is documented in Acts 7. He preached from Genesis to his present day, revealing God as the God of glory, the God who appeared to Abraham and led him out from Ur. He spoke of the Abrahamic covenant and the lives of Jacob, Joseph and Moses. He described the release of the Israelites from Egypt and their wilderness wanderings. He reminded his listeners of the idolatry of the Israelites while in the wilderness, and how the Lord commanded that they erect a Tabernacle. He explained how Joshua dispossessed the nations in the Promised Land, and how David desired to build a permanent dwelling place for God.

Then Stephen began to sum up his dissertation, explaining that the Most High does not live in a structure:

> But it was Solomon who built a house for Him. However, the Most High does not dwell in houses and temples made with hands; as the prophet says, Heaven [is] My throne, and earth the footstool for My feet. What [kind of] house can you build for Me, says the Lord, or what is the place in which I can rest? Was it not My hand that made all these things? You stubborn and stiff-necked people, still heathen and uncircumcised in heart and ears, you are always actively resisting the Holy Spirit. As your forefathers [were], so you [are and so you do]! Which of the prophets did your fathers not persecute? And they slew those who proclaimed beforehand the coming of the Righteous One, Whom you now have betrayed and murdered—you who received the Law as it was ordained and set in order and delivered by angels, and [yet] you did not obey it!
>
> Acts 7:47–53 AMPLIFIED

Imagine how angry the Sanhedrin became as they heard truth that opposed their mindsets and doctrines. While they did not dispute Stephen's words concerning the history of their faith, when he preached about Christ and how He lives in us and we in Him, great opposition arose.

The Sanhedrin, therefore, their minds limited by "religion," wanted to kill Stephen for preaching truth.

How Religion Infuriates!

When the Jews heard these things they were "cut to the heart and infuriated, and they ground their teeth against [Stephen]" (Acts 7:54 AMPLIFIED). What infuriated them? It was the fact that their holy Temple built by human hands (and the beauty that they created in it) was not where God wanted to dwell. All of their religious practices did nothing to invite God into their midst. The Most High does not dwell in houses and temples made by human hands.

In addition, Stephen, speaking for God, called them stiff-necked people. He then called them heathens—uncircumcised in their hearts and ears, resisting the Holy Spirit. To be referred to as heathen was a slap in the face to the Jews, since heathens were considered both ungodly and unclean—and the Jews took great care in their cleansing rituals. They did not allow outward defilement of any kind; the unclean were forbidden to enter the house of the Lord.

The Jews had denied the Righteous One: Christ Jesus. They depended upon strict observance of the Law to make them righteous. But Stephen was pointing out that our righteousness is in Christ, not in the works of our own hands. Righteousness is available to us through Christ alone, and the power of God is rooted in His righteousness. (This is still an issue in the Church, and we will discuss it at length later.)

Stephen finished speaking and, still full of and led by the Holy Spirit, saw the glory of God: "Look! I see the heavens opened and the Son of Man standing at the right hand of God!" (Acts 7:56 NKJV).

The Sanhedrin did not want to hear it. "Yelling at the top of their voices," they covered their ears. They were so enraged that "they all rushed at him, dragged him out of the city and began to stone him" (Acts 7:57–58).

Thus, the garments of the persecutors ended up at the feet of Saul.

> And they stoned Stephen as he was calling on God and saying, "Lord Jesus, receive my spirit." Then he knelt down and cried out with a loud voice, "Lord, do not charge them with this sin." And when he had said this, he fell asleep.
>
> Acts 7:59–60 NKJV

Hungry for the Supernatural

Legalism. Pharisaism. Religion. These spirits did not die in the first century. Fueled by a spirit of Antichrist that denies the finished work of Christ at the cross, they continue to hinder us as we attempt to move in God's power. Indeed, these demonic spirits are assigned to the Church to keep us bound in a "works mentality." Just as these spirits targeted Stephen, so they target those today who demonstrate God's Spirit and power.

And they spawn other evil spirits, including two that may surprise you: guilt and shame. Yes, guilt and shame keep us from flowing in the supernatural—but they were conquered by Jesus at the cross. Perfectionism is another spirit strongly connected to legalism that keeps us from flowing in God's power. As we continue you will see that you are washed as white as snow, and God wants to use you. You are created in the image of Christ; your spirit is perfect, for you are clothed with His righteousness.

Dear one, commit to walking with me. On this journey you will be empowered to have faith and grace to walk in the supernatural. I am certain that God will lead us into all truth and revelation as we seek to access His power.

You did not pick up this book by mistake. You are like me and others who are hungry to experience God's power. We are all hungry for the supernatural. I am not referring to a spooky spiritual experience or another emotional high. I am referring to having the mind of God and seeing beyond what we see in the natural, all of which involves moving past anything that limits us.

Let me assure you:

- God is performing miracles today. He is the same yesterday, today and forever.
- God wants to use you now to demonstrate His power on earth (see Matthew 10:8).
- You are already righteous in Christ Jesus; therefore, God's resurrection power can and does already flow in you and through you.

And one more thing: It is important for you to know how much God loves you. He wants you to know the power of His resurrection. Read the following passage silently, and then read it again aloud, declaring God's Word and receiving it by faith.

[May I] be found in Him, not having my own righteousness, which is from the law, but that which is through faith in Christ, the righteousness which is from God by faith; that I may know Him and the power of His resurrection, and the fellowship of His sufferings, being conformed to His death.

Philippians 3:9–10 NKJV

Now, precious believer, you have decreed that you will know Him and the power of His resurrection. God is promising to release His mantle of power over you. As we move forward, He will deliver you from anything that hinders you from moving in that awesome, transforming power.

2

The Transformation of a Legalist

Letting Go of Pride

S aul, the legalist, was about to be changed. He could never have imagined at this stage, having just witnessed the stoning of Stephen, that he would ever lay down his pride in his religious zeal. Yet look at these words he wrote some years later to the church at Corinth:

> For you see your calling, brethren, that not many wise according to the flesh, not many mighty, not many noble, are called. But God has *chosen the foolish things* of the world to put to shame the wise, and God has *chosen the weak things* of the world to put to shame the things which are mighty; and the base things of the world and the things which are despised God has chosen, and the things which are not, to bring to nothing the things that are, that no flesh should glory in His presence. But of Him you are in Christ Jesus, who became for us wisdom from God—and righteousness and sanctification and redemption—that, as it is written, "He who glories, let him glory in the LORD."
>
> 1 Corinthians 1:26–31 NKJV (emphasis added)

Foolish. Wow! Might not Saul—now known as Paul—be revealing something about himself here, admitting that "foolish things" exposed his own boasting and self-righteousness? (Note: Most historians agree that Saul was his Jewish name; he later received the name of Paul as recognition of his Roman citizenship. See also Acts 13:9.)

Now that is a word to ponder: God uses *foolish* things to confound human wisdom. That word *foolish* used in this passage is the Greek word *moros*, and it has two definitions. One definition is "dull and stupid." Another, now please brace yourself, is "blockhead and absurd." Hmmm. My mind is whirling as I think of all of the blockhead things I have done in my life, and that just maybe God was there—trying to get my attention. I know for a fact that I had a tendency in my past to think legalistically and even to minister in the same fashion. Thanks to God's grace I am now a different person. I understand that I am righteous *only* because of the blood of Jesus. I never have to prove my value to anyone. Scripture says that I am seated with Christ in heavenly places.

I may be preaching to the choir right now, but let me assure you that most of us are blind to the way pride limits us from moving forward in power. Pride will never allow us to recognize our need for a Savior; it will always hide the fact that we cannot earn our own righteousness. Because of that, God will often allow some absurd situations to occur. We may encounter circumstances in which we are "set up" to appear foolish. Not to hurt us—that is not God's heart. We must always remember *who* the true Teacher is: The Holy Spirit is the Teacher, not our trials or temptations. But He will allow us to experience "opportunities" that turn our hearts toward Him—sometimes to the point where we can do nothing but cry out to Him.

If you have not noticed, crying out to God is what all Christians have in common. He allows us to fail so that in times when we try to follow all the *rules* (being "under the Law" of the Old Testament), we realize that there is no possible way to be righteous enough or good enough for God to bless us.

But perhaps as you are reading, you are receiving further revelation—that even though we may feel completely unworthy, hopeless, dull and foolish, God still loves us and desires to use us to show His glory. He desires, in fact, to reveal His glory *in* and *through* each of us. Our problems come when we are wise in our own eyes, seeking satisfaction from our personal achievements—in other words, proud of our religious works or intellectual achievement.

Please do not misunderstand me: I fully embrace the importance of walking in wisdom. We are encouraged by Scripture to seek wisdom. There are, however, evil spirits connected to pride that rob us of godly power. Make no mistake about it: This book intends to teach you to tear down those strongholds that limit you from demonstrating God's power.

God's Unusual Choices

Look again at 1 Corinthians 1:27. It points out clearly that God *has chosen the foolish things* to shame the wise; God *has chosen the weak things* to shame the strong. Paul went on to write that God has also chosen base or lowly things and despised things—even things that are not—in order to bring to nothing the things that are. *Now we can ask:*

For what purpose? In verse 29 we discover the reason: He does this so that no one may boast before Him.

No one could have written this passage more appropriately than the apostle Paul. You will realize why in a few minutes. For now, focus on this interesting fact: God Himself has *chosen*. Imagine God on the throne desiring to empower someone like Saul who took such pride in his religion; a man who had studied under exemplary rabbis and knew the Torah well; a man who had approved of the stoning of Stephen and who was persecuting the fledgling Church. Think of all that Saul was doing in the name of religious pride and arrogance. And yet, as God knew what was in the heart of Saul and mankind in general, He *chose* to use *foolish things* to confound the wise . . . or those who thought they were wise. In other words, as we will see in a moment, God chose a "blockhead" named Saul.

The word *chosen* in the original Greek is *eklegomai*, (pronounced ek-*leg*-om-ahee) and it means "to select; to make one's favorite." This implies that it was God's *first* choice to use foolish things to confound the wise, although He probably had many different choices available. Understanding this, we can conclude that God's original intent was to use what was foolish in order to confound (or put to shame) those who considered themselves wise.

A biblical word study connects the word *wise* to the Greek word *phronimos* (pronounced *fron*-ee-mos), which is connected to "being thoughtful and acquiring mental intellect"— a simple and familiar definition. In a negative sense, however, it is connected to the word *conceited*. We have all known people who have a haughty opinion of themselves. Yes, it is disgusting. Just imagine how it hurts the heart of God.

But have we truly allowed the eyes of our own hearts to open enough to recognize our own pride and arrogance? Let's be honest: We are *all* prideful—especially if we believe that we can perform properly to persuade God to love us enough to fulfill His promises. Religious works are dead works; they get us no extra points with God. Only the blood of Jesus gains us entrance into the presence of God, and only because of Him are we promised victory.

This is where Saul came into the picture. He was prideful and conceited, and I have always believed that God had to knock him off his "high horse" to get his attention.

The Road to Deliverance

Most Christians know the story of Saul's conversion on the road to Damascus. Acts 9:3–4 describes his experience: "As he journeyed he came near Damascus, and suddenly a light shone around him from heaven. Then he fell to the ground, and heard a voice saying to him, 'Saul, Saul, why are you persecuting Me?'" (NKJV). There are two other accounts of Saul's conversion in Scripture, which he gave during times of public defense (see Acts 22, which we will explore in the next chapter, and Acts 26).

Saul was most likely on a horse (some theologians suggest a camel), and he fell to the ground upon encountering Jesus. Go ahead, get a visual of this: Saul was knocked down from his high opinion of himself and the pride of his theology.

I remember when I was a child and my father, Bud Davis, would give me instruction. As a child who desired her own way (yes, I can be stubborn—even now), I began to rebel. One day I found myself digging in—you know, taking a firm stand and preparing to defend my position. Then, like a cannon firing, the words *No! I'm* not *going to stay in for lunch to rest. I am going out to play!* exploded from my mouth.

Well, I will refrain from describing the look in my dad's eyes, but his words were: "Sandra Kay Davis" (he always used my full name during correction), "you'd better come down off your *high horse* right now!"

Even then I understood what a "high horse" was. Today I am even more aware of times when I climb up to a lofty place and insist on having my own way. Too bad for Saul. He was blinded by his pride—in fact, he felt as if he was doing God a favor by murdering Christians. His deception cost him dearly. His spiritual pride was dwarfed by God, and he was struck blind. It was that very incident, however, that changed this persecutor of Christians into the world's foremost evangelist of the Good News.

More Foolishness Revealed

The first mention of Saul's conversion, written by Luke in Acts 9, is given not in the form of testimony, but rather as documentation of his encounter with Jesus. Take some time and read through it. Again, pay attention to the italicized words:

> Meanwhile Saul, still drawing his breath hard from threatening and murderous desire against the disciples of the Lord, went to the high priest and *requested* of him letters to the synagogues at Damascus [*authorizing him*], so that if he found any men or women belonging to the Way [of life as determined by faith in Jesus Christ], *he might bring them bound* [*with chains*] *to Jerusalem.*

Now as he traveled on, he came near to Damascus, and suddenly a light from heaven flashed around him, and *he fell* to the ground. Then he heard a voice saying to him, Saul, Saul, why are you persecuting Me [harassing, troubling, and molesting Me]?

And Saul said, Who are You, Lord? And He said, I am Jesus, Whom you are persecuting. *It is dangerous and it will turn out badly for you to keep kicking against the goad [to offer vain and perilous resistance].*

Trembling and astonished he asked, Lord, what do You desire me to do? The Lord said to him, But arise and go into the city, and *you will be told what you must do.* The men who were accompanying him were unable to speak [for terror], hearing the voice but seeing no one.

Then Saul got up from the ground, but though his eyes were opened, he could see nothing; *so they led him by the hand and brought him into Damascus. And he was unable to see for three days, and he neither ate nor drank [anything].*

Now there was in Damascus a disciple named Ananias. The Lord said to him in a vision, Ananias. And he answered, Here am I, Lord. And the Lord said to him, Get up and go to the street called Straight and ask at the house of Judas for a man of Tarsus named Saul, for behold, he is praying [there]. And he has seen in a vision a man named Ananias enter and lay his hands on him so that he might regain his sight.

But Ananias answered, Lord, I have heard many people tell about this man, especially how much evil and what great suffering he has brought on Your saints at Jerusalem; now he is here and has authority from the high priests to put in chains all who call upon Your name.

But the Lord said to him, Go, *for this man is a chosen instrument of Mine* to bear My name before the Gentiles and kings and the descendants of Israel; *for I will make*

*clear to him how much he will be afflicted and must endure
and suffer for My name's sake.*

So Ananias left and went into the house. And he laid
his hands on Saul and said, Brother Saul, the Lord Jesus,
Who appeared to you along the way by which you came
here, has sent me that you may recover your sight and be
filled with the Holy Spirit. And instantly something like
scales fell from [Saul's] eyes, and he recovered his sight.
Then he arose and was baptized.

And after he took some food, he was strengthened. For
several days [afterward] he remained with the disciples at
Damascus. And immediately in the synagogues he proclaimed Jesus, saying, He is the Son of God!

And all who heard him were amazed and said, Is not this
the very man who harassed and overthrew and destroyed
in Jerusalem those who called upon this Name? And he
has come here for the express purpose of arresting them
and bringing them in chains before the chief priests. But
Saul increased all the more in strength, and continued to
confound and put to confusion the Jews who lived in Damascus by comparing and examining evidence and proving
that Jesus is the Christ (the Messiah).

Acts 9:1–22 AMPLIFIED (emphasis added)

Here we see Saul's pride, asking for letters from authorities for him to persecute the Christians—to bind them in
chains and put them on trial for heresy. Let me plead my
case concerning how God allows some foolish things to
happen to arrest our hearts:

Point Number One: God is the Judge and the only one to
release judgment. He sits in the seat of judgment—not
Saul, ourselves or others. Not even Bible scholars.

Point Number Two: Saul fell. How foolish he looked! When he realized just whom he was persecuting— well, you can imagine him thinking to himself, *I've been so foolish. I've been such a blockhead.*

Point Number Three: Saul was trembling. He probably appeared as if he were experiencing a seizure. Imagine again Saul jerking, trembling blindly as he attempted to locate the voice speaking to him. Imagine those watching. Not only were they fearful, but they also were looking at someone who until this time was rigidly in control and was now acting like a lunatic.

Point Number Four: Saul's eyes were opened, but he could not see. How weird is that? Might someone say, "Saul, you're really being ludicrous today. Falling off your horse, acting like a maniac and experiencing wide-eyed blindness."

Point Number Five: Saul, this great man of power who bound others in chains and dragged them to persecution, was now weak, blind and had to be led by others to a place he had never been. He was out of control— something prideful people fail to deal with well!

Point Number Six: God spoke to Ananias, a Christian in Damascus, and told him to go lay hands on Saul—the man who had come to arrest believers like himself. How foolish could that seem? In these times God is choosing the irrational things to confound the wise— those who feel as if they have God figured out and expect Him to conform to their religious mindsets. Still, try to imagine more of the conversation written between the lines:

ANANIAS: Uh, God, uh, I want to be obedient, but don't You think it would be imprudent for me to go to Saul? After all, he has come to destroy all of us who belong to The Way.

GOD: We are not considering your own wisdom here. I am taking what appears foolish and overshadowing your own natural wisdom with My divine plan and purpose. I desire to use you to demonstrate My power, and when Saul is healed, he will be used to do the same for others.

Paul Becomes "Unmade"

In this first scriptural account of Paul's conversion, he was the persecutor. In the two later accounts, he was the persecuted. God unmade him. Yes, once we meet Jesus we become like Isaiah and find that we are "undone" or basically "unmade" (see Isaiah 6:5). What we were no longer exists when we meet our Savior and become transformed.

Meeting Jesus so changed Paul that he abandoned the foolishness of pride and began to live only for the sake of ministering the Gospel of the Kingdom. I believe his prayer might have been something like this:

Lord, I was a foolish man until I found Jesus Christ. I am thankful that You have saved me. I now want to be a testimony for Your glory. I want those who are lost to know the saving power of Jesus Christ. I forfeit any right to consider how foolish I might feel at this point. You have surpassed my own intelligence with Your godly wisdom. You have always known the right path for my life. Allow me to share my testimony—surely someone will hear it and say, "Do that for me, Lord Jesus. Save me from my sins. Open my eyes so that I can see. Allow the scales to fall from my eyes so that I can see You as You are."

Foolish? Actually, yes and no. It all depends how it is used by the Father. I will be a fool for Him, and yet I want Him to allow some of my foolish mistakes to awaken me, to cleanse and purify me. Remaining puffy is not much fun—remaining puffed up is definitely not in our future. Let's decide right now to allow Him to transform us more into His divine image.

Remember you are chosen. We will stand eternally with the King of kings clothed in His righteousness. Though we are spiritually at war, we, along with the Lamb (the Chosen and Faithful One), triumph:

> They will wage war against the Lamb, and the Lamb will triumph over them; for He is Lord of lords and King of kings—and those with Him and on His side are chosen and called [elected] and loyal and faithful followers.
>
> Revelation 17:14 AMPLIFIED

Time for Reflection

1. Do you believe you serve a God who is harsh, hard and condemning? Maybe you think that is why Paul got knocked off his "high horse." If so, I am so excited you are reading this book. A message concerning God's love means just that—*love*! Scripture tells us that God *is* love. He is not waiting for you to mess up so that He can smack you. Is this how you see God when you think about Him—or when you feel you have not measured up to your personal standard of holiness or righteousness?

2. Take a moment and write down a time (or times) that you have felt that way.

_____

_____

_____

_____

3. Now, let's back up a moment and look at what the Word says about being convicted of sin. The Gospel of John tells us that the Holy Spirit will convict (reprove) the "world" of sin. The "world" indicates those who are not believers: He convicts *unbelievers* of their sins; *believers* are convicted of their righteousness. Read the passage below:

And when he is come, he will reprove the world of sin, and of righteousness, and of judgment: of sin, because they believe not on me; of righteousness, because I go to my Father, and ye see me no more; of judgment, because the prince of this world is judged.

John 16:8–11 KJV

Let me clarify something here. The Holy Spirit assures us of our righteousness in Christ. Because of this wonderful knowledge, we desire to obey Jesus, and that is why we repent when we sin. Think of it this way: If Christ lives in us, then why would we want to do anything that would grieve Him? Scripture says that we are not to grieve the Holy Spirit. Since the Godhead is One—God the Father, God the Son and God the Holy Spirit—then I do not desire to put myself in any ungodly environment. That is why I shun sin—not because I am afraid He is waiting to punish me whenever I mess up, but because I love Him. This way of thinking removes us from an unhealthy, prideful view of God.

38

Precious reader, please hear my heart when I state that it is my assessment that the world is still laboring under Law—trying to achieve righteousness on its own. It is as if we believe that we can be *good enough* or *righteous enough* to be holy and acceptable.

The Holy Spirit convicts unbelievers of their sinfulness and need for a Savior, but believers are convicted of our righteousness in Jesus. The Holy Spirit challenges the hearts of mankind and asks: "Do you believe you are holy and righteous because of what you *do* for Me?" If the answer is yes, He begins to point out that we have attempted to place religious works above the finished work of Christ at the cross.

Paul addressed the Galatians concerning this matter of righteousness (see Galatians 3). The Galatian church began with faith in God and the understanding that they were righteous due to the shed blood of Jesus. Later, however, they fell backward under the burden of the Law, which completely negated the finished work of the cross.

It all begins in our hearts now, because we are under a New Covenant; we are no longer judged according to the Law. God's laws are written on our hearts; therefore, our hearts are our consciences, and they will lead us to repentance when we sin.

Judgment is mentioned in this Scripture because Jesus was judged on our behalf. He paid the ultimate sacrifice at the cross. The Law was given to God's people to show that we need a Savior; until Jesus came no one could fulfill its requirements.

Genesis 1:1 says, "In the beginning God." This means the fullness of the Godhead—Father, Son and Holy Spirit—worked together from the foundation of the world. Jesus knew as the worlds were framed that His destiny involved the cross. With that in mind, can you see yourself forgiven? If you have fallen into the religious trap of trying to measure up to God's standards, repent (which means to change the mind, to turn away from the sin). Then turn your thoughts to your righteousness in Christ. Your sin of pride is forgiven. Begin to focus on this fact: *I am the righteousness of Christ; I am a new creation in Christ Jesus.*

These confessions, below, will help confirm your identity in Christ. Take time to ponder them:

- I am a born-again believer. I have access to the throne of God.
- I can run boldly to the throne and allow God to wrap His arms around me when I need help or comfort.
- I am righteous because Christ shed His blood, which covers my sin—past, present and future.
- Every day and in every way Christ in me is causing my life to be better—filled with His joy and life.
- Christ in me is my hope of glory!

Here is my prayer for you:

Father God, I am so grateful that we are gaining greater understanding of who we are in Christ, and that we are already righteous because of the finished work of Christ at the cross. Thank You for setting us free from a spirit of condemnation and death. I pray that our eyes will be opened to Your truth and that we will walk in the fullness of Your Spirit and the newness of life through Christ Jesus. In the mighty name of Jesus I pray, Amen.

3

When the Going Gets Rough

Letting Go of Pressure to Achieve Results

We see thus far in the story of Paul's life that suddenly the shoe was on the other foot. The biggest battle after the conversion of this legalist seemed to be against a spirit of legalism. Maybe you experienced the same opposition once you received Christ as your own personal Savior.

Allow me to interject this thought based upon personal experience: Once you understand that God does not expect religious works or performance (or perfection apart from Christ), an ugly spirit of legalism will rise up to oppose your every step toward being transformed. After all, this revelation empowers you to break through your limitations and experience more of His power. Is it any wonder the enemy wants to keep us blinded to the truth that we are no longer under the Law?

Scripture says that the Holy Spirit makes alive (see 2 Corinthians 3:6). This does not mean that, as we step forth and demonstrate God's power on earth, we will not face opposition. In fact, the more we attempt to minister the New Covenant, the more opposition we will face.

Paul, again, is our teacher. He entered the mission field with the same fervor with which he had persecuted believers. And no matter the opposition, he persevered. His list of hardships makes my Christian walk as mere marshmallows. In his second letter to the Corinthian church, Paul outlined some of the experiences he endured in order to preach the Gospel.

> From the Jews five times I received forty stripes minus one. Three times I was beaten with rods; once I was stoned; three times I was shipwrecked; a night and a day I have been in the deep; in journeys often, in perils of waters, in perils of robbers, in perils of my own countrymen, in perils of the Gentiles, in perils in the city, in perils in the wilderness, in perils in the sea, in perils among false brethren; in weariness and toil, in sleeplessness often, in hunger and thirst, in fastings often, in cold and nakedness—besides the other things, what comes upon me daily: my deep concern for all the churches.
>
> 2 Corinthians 11:24–28

Fausset's Bible Dictionary describes the "perils of waters" as danger in fording rivers at flood stage, bridges being a rarity. It also suggests that Paul's "thorn in the flesh," which he mentions in 2 Corinthians 12:7, was "probably some painful, tedious, bodily malady, which shamed him before those to whom he ministered." And Paul mentions still "other things" that came upon him daily!

Though some may believe that Paul's thorn in the flesh was as *Fausset's* describes, 2 Corinthians 12:7 describes it as a "messenger of Satan" sent to buffet Paul. Why would God allow this? To keep Paul from becoming "puffed up." If you remember, 1 Corinthians 8:1–3 says, "Knowledge puffs up, but love builds up. The man who thinks he knows something does not yet know as he ought to know. But the man who loves God is known by God." Is it possible that God sent an evil messenger to Paul so that the fruit of love could be grown in Paul's heart and ministry? Any of us can take pride in knowledge, but do we possess His love and demonstrate it? To demonstrate love also demonstrates His power!

Yes, there is much to learn concerning how evil spirits will try to persecute us as we turn from legalism and walk in the demonstration and power of God. And persecution can take many forms; our enemy is cunning. His opposition is not always what we might expect. In this chapter we are going to take a look at an experience of opposition that basically left Paul speechless. And we will conclude this chapter with the meaning of testimony—which overcomes the often defeating feeling of being ineffective in our witnessing. Telling our stories of Jesus' work in our lives lifts the false pressure of having to prove ourselves and sets our hearts free.

Hitting the Wall at Mars Hill

Paul experienced not only hardships during his missionary work, as noted above, but also the miraculous. These experiences gave Paul a platform for speaking to every audience he encountered. The life of Paul leaves us with an unforgettable impression of how he was humbled by God in the beginning, and how he moved in the power of the Holy Spirit everywhere he traveled throughout his life . . . *except* when he preached to the Greek intelligentsia at Mars Hill. Paul welcomed a challenge to enter a debate with this elite gathering, but he accomplished little.

What blocked his ministry there? Grab a pen and paper and take notes as we go to document anything that quickens your spirit, any area where the Holy Spirit reveals something that limits you from fulfilling His call on your life. We will address many potential strongholds along the way. We will see that demonstrating the power of God is not about how much head knowledge we have accumulated, or how much of the Bible (or the Law) we can recite. Knowing Christ as our Savior is what empowers us to do as He has commanded—to heal the sick, raise the dead, cast out demons. Read below how He has commissioned us.

> And He appointed twelve to continue to be with Him, and that He might send them out to preach [as apostles or special messengers] and to have authority and power to heal the sick and to drive out demons.
>
> Mark 3:14–15 AMPLIFIED

> These twelve Jesus sent forth, and charged them, saying, Go not into the way of the Gentiles, and into any city of the Samaritans enter ye not. But go rather to the lost sheep of the house of Israel. And as ye go, preach, saying, The kingdom of heaven is at hand. Heal the sick, cleanse the lepers, raise the dead, cast out devils: freely ye have received, freely give.
>
> Matthew 10:5–8 KJV

Then He called His twelve disciples together and gave them power and authority over all demons, and to cure diseases. He sent them to preach the kingdom of God and to heal the sick.

Luke 9:1–2 NKJV

As you continue to read, please keep in mind that I am not in any way saying that we all have to go through what Paul did to be used of God. The point is that when we came to Christ, we died to ourselves. It is true that we are to die daily and also that we will suffer persecution. Dying to self, however, is not some type of martyr syndrome—where we continually put ourselves down and even expect God to put us down. Quite the contrary. I look at dying daily as dying to limitations I have placed upon myself or that I have taken on by believing the lies of the enemy.

My old, limited nature died when I met Christ, and every day my old nature continues to remain dead. To die to self is simply to die to my old life. Persecution will come in many forms. Jesus warned us about times of persecution; however, I do not view these as times that I am being punished or even a part of dying to self. I view persecution as an opportunity to remind myself that I am royalty, God's ambassador on earth, and nothing can rob me of my God-given identity.

Determined Again to Teach the Gospel

Let's look at Paul's travels leading to Mars Hill. Paul began to preach in the synagogues "at once" after his eyes were opened (Acts 9:20). We read that "Saul grew more and more powerful and baffled the Jews living in Damascus by proving that Jesus is the Christ" (Acts 9:22). He began his ministry travels and spoke boldly wherever he went.

Acts 17 begins with Paul and Silas, a prophet whom Paul had chosen as a fellow worker, entering Thessalonica. Paul, as usual, went straight to the synagogue of the Jews to preach. For three Sabbaths he "reasoned" and "argued" with them from the Scriptures. He attempted to explain to them that it was necessary for Christ to suffer and rise from the dead—thus proving that Jesus is the Christ, the Messiah. Some of them believed and began to associate themselves with Paul and Silas, as well as a great number of devout Greeks (following Christ) and many important women in the city.

The unbelieving Jews, however, were provoked to jealousy and gathered together an angry mob causing a great uproar. They went to the house of Jason demanding he bring Paul and Silas out to them. When they were unable to find Paul and Silas, they attacked the house of Jason and dragged him and some of the brethren before the city authorities, complaining that Paul and Silas were troublemakers and that Jason had housed the duo. They proclaimed that everywhere Paul and Silas went they "turned the world upside down" (Acts 17:6), and now they were trying to do the same in their city.

Let's pause. I love the fact that two men of God were turning the world upside down. This is what a Christian free from the bondage of limitations and full of the power and demonstration of the Spirit of God is meant to do! Reader, this is a time to ponder: Maybe if we were as committed as Paul and Silas, we would be witnessing the supernatural in a more tangible way. Or, put another way, we would be witnessing "heaven on earth." Remember, Jesus brought His world with Him when He came to save us. He wants us to demonstrate God's power on earth.

To be forewarned is to be forearmed. The enemy may try to stop us, but God's grace is always sufficient. So go ahead, imagine yourself tearing down false kingdoms and every high thing that attempts to exalt itself above the knowledge of God. It is in you to do these things—you are chosen.

Okay, back to the angry mob. The mob declared that these believers were acting contrary to the decrees of Caesar and were asserting that there was another king, Jesus. Well, the crowd caused the city authorities to be stirred up also. So, the city magistrate received the bail for Jason and some of the brethren and let them go. Paul and Silas were sent away safely by night to Berea.

As soon as they arrived in the new town, as you might guess, Paul and Silas located another synagogue. Believer, think about this. They barely escaped being bound in chains, maybe even stoning, and they looked immediately for another place to preach the Good News.

In Berea, the Jews were "more fair-minded than those in Thessalonica" (Acts 17:11). They were actually ready for the Good News and accepted and welcomed the message concerning Christ, salvation and the Kingdom of God. The Amplified version states it this way:

> Now these [Jews] were better disposed and more noble than those in Thessalonica, for they were entirely ready and accepted and welcomed the message [concerning the attainment through Christ of eternal salvation in the kingdom

of God] with inclination of mind and eagerness, searching and examining the Scriptures daily to see if these things were so. Many of them therefore became believers, together with not a few prominent Greeks, women as well as men.

Acts 17:11–12 AMPLIFIED

Opposition Once More

I believe you have a good idea of all that Paul and Silas were experiencing as they spread the Gospel. Imagine yourself against an angry mob. If you escaped would you be so eager to preach right away? Oh, my! Studying this is truly humbling. Much of this chapter has been written with tears flowing. It makes me wonder: *If God chose Paul, who was "foolish," can He also actually use me?* We reflect on this fact once again: All the grace needed is supplied when we are chosen of God.

Scripture teaches us of others who felt weak and un-qualified—Moses, Gideon, David. The natural man (especially a Pharisee) would not pay any attention to someone who could not speak well or was not counted among the learned. All I can say at this point is that with God all things are possible. For Him to use this five-foot-two-inch Texas gal to minister publicly and write books for Him is amazing to me. So often I feel foolish attempting to put my thoughts on paper. I often voice to my husband, "Who would ever want to read what I have to say?" I admit, I do have a *big mouth*, and I have preached under the anointing and inspiration of the Holy Spirit, but still I wonder.

Scripture tells us this about what happens when God chooses and uses us:

You know that the household of Stephanas were the first converts in Achaia, and they have *devoted* themselves to the service of the saints. I urge you, brothers, to submit to such as these and to everyone who joins in the work, and labors at it.

1 Corinthians 16:15–16 (emphasis added)

The word *devoted* in this passage also means "addicted." Maybe that is what Paul experienced—an addiction to minister the Gospel. After all, we are encouraged to be that way. I consider being addicted to ministry a needed asset as I testify of His glory. I bet you are sensing the same.

Let's keep reading. Expect to leave behind the limitation of feeling ineffective in your calling, because God desires to use you in a mighty way . . . even to turn the world upside down:

When the Jews from Thessalonica learned that the word of God was preached by Paul at Berea, they came there also and stirred up the crowds. Then immediately the brethren sent Paul away, to go to the sea; but both Silas and Timothy remained there. So those who conducted Paul brought him to Athens; and receiving a command for Silas and Timothy to come to him with all speed, they departed. . . . Now while Paul waited for them at Athens, his spirit was provoked within him [greatly grieved] when he saw that the city was given over to idols.

Acts 17:13–14, 16 NKJV

So, guess where Paul headed next? Yes! To the synagogue to address the Jews and the Gentiles who worshiped there. He did not stop there, though; he headed also to the marketplace to preach the Good News. This got the attention of the Epicurean and Stoic philosophers, which led to his sermon on Mars Hill. Up until now Paul had been turning the world upside down. In his next encounter, however, his world of influence seemed to take a nosedive. Let's read how and why.

The Mars Hill Encounter

Picture the setting. Among the rocky hills of Athens, northwest of the Acropolis, was Mars Hill, better known as the Areopagus. It was here that the Athenian judicial council met. On the Acropolis itself stood the famous Parthenon, the temple dedicated to the worship of the idol Athena. (Many other false gods were worshiped in Athens—especially Diana—but this temple was dedicated to Athena.)

It is interesting that, like most Greek temples, the Parthenon was also used as a treasury. So I believe it is safe to say that when Paul entered Athens, he was prayerfully opposing not only idolatry, but also the spirit of Mammon. If you remember, it was here that Paul and Silas cast a demon out of a slave girl who was involved in witchcraft. Her owners were so upset (because of the income lost when her ability to tell fortunes ended) that they had Paul and Silas thrown in prison.

Greek mythology places Mars Hill as the scene of the trial of the god Mars, who was accused of murdering one of the other Greek god's sons. Sixteen stone steps in the rock bed, which still exist today, rise from the valley up to Mars Hill. Benches of stones were cut into the rock in this valley. It was here that the Greek judges sat to determine criminal and religious cases—in the open air.

The one accused sat on two crude blocks (still seen today): one on the east and the other on the west. Here sat Paul disputing with Greek philosophers as if he were on trial. Well, considering what the area was used for—he was!

They brought him up from below, step by step, and seated him on the benches. It was here that Paul made an impressive speech, a memorable address, which has impressed scholars through the centuries. It is obvious that Paul "knew his stuff." His allusions to their culture, his observations and logical conclusions, and his intense, earnest oration stood in direct contrast to their love of wisdom for its own sake. Believing themselves to be of superior intellect, they were, still, quite impressed with Paul. As persuasive as Paul was, however, there was no melting of the hearts in the crowd. In fact, only a few people were saved while he was in Athens.

Now this occurred, remember, after Paul was criticized by his detractors for "turning the world upside down." Yet, when he spoke in the midst of a stronghold of intellectualism and humanism, he made little impact. Why was that? Read on!

Preachers' Blue Mondays

Forty years ago my pastor spoke about having "Blue Mondays." At the time, I had no idea what he meant—except that I did not desire to experience one of those. I learned, years later, that it is a term preachers use when Monday rolls around after a particularly vibrant Sunday service. I have now had Blue Mondays myself. Generally this refers to times not only of exhaustion from the ministry on Sunday, but a huge letdown after experiencing powerful anointing the day before. Nothing compares to being under the anointing of God. One might equate the letdown afterward to having a glorious two-week vacation on a tropical isle and then returning to the office on Monday morning.

There is another type of Blue Monday—the day when you recall what you preached on Sunday and wish it could have turned out better. These types of Blue Mondays cause us to second-guess ourselves. Our enemy, the accuser, really hits hard on days like this. These are times to examine our hearts, our ministries, and to allow the Lord to speak to us concerning what His will was for that time of service.

After Paul left Athens, he went to Corinth. I believe that in his journey to the next city, he went through a soul-searching process—much like a Blue Monday. Surely he had given the best speech possible to those philosophers. Yes, he had been prepared. He had spoken accurately, even correctly. He had been primed, pumped and properly positioned to speak "for God." Maybe he felt, as I often have, that he had to "prove" the truth to others. What pressure that is!

Ultimately, all of his intellect did little for the Kingdom, as only a few were saved. I feel sure that Paul recognized this and spent some time reviewing his ministry in Athens. There was ample time to replay his words in his mind on the way to Corinth. I would bet that he went over his encounter with the Athenians many, many times. It is quite obvious that he had a change of heart by the time he arrived in Corinth.

Why do I say that? My answer is that he told the Corinthians that he was weak, fearful and trembling as he came into their city. The great orator wrote that he "did not come with excellence of speech or of wisdom" (see 1 Corinthians 2:1–3 NKJV). He told how he had not come to them puffed up or full of pride. In fact he stated:

> As for myself, brethren, when I came to you, I did not come proclaiming to you the testimony and evidence or mystery and secret of God [concerning what He has done through Christ for the salvation of men] in lofty words of eloquence or human philosophy and wisdom; for I resolved to know nothing (to be acquainted with nothing, to make a display of the knowledge of nothing, and to be conscious of nothing) among you except Jesus Christ (the Messiah) and Him crucified.
>
> And I was in (passed into a state of) weakness and fear (dread) and great trembling [after I had come] among you. And my language and my message were not set forth in persuasive (enticing and plausible) words of wisdom, but they were in demonstration of the [Holy] Spirit and power [a proof by the Spirit and power of God, operating on me and stirring in the minds of my hearers the most holy emotions and thus persuading them], so that your faith might not rest in the wisdom of men (human philosophy), but in the power of God.
>
> 1 Corinthians 2:1–5 AMPLIFIED

Did you notice that Paul took no credit for his own wisdom and knowledge? He explained that he came as if he knew nothing except the fact of "Jesus Christ and Him crucified." Paul was weak, fearful and trembling while among them. He was also concerned that people would put their faith in the wisdom of men rather than trusting God.

Now, some interpret this to mean that Paul was exhausted and possibly ill. I think not. I think he learned a valuable lesson at Mars Hill. He probably concluded that if you just teach about the goodness of God (and the finished work of Christ) and teach with a pure heart—rather than focus on the excellence of oration—then the miracles will come.

Please do not misunderstand this teacher of the Word. Believe me, I study . . . a lot. I prepare my messages in outline form, using PowerPoint and handouts if I need to. I have learned, however, that it is not about *what* I know as much as it is about *whom* I know. In my own strength, I can do nothing. There is not a time when I stand before a congregation that I do not completely lean on Him. Inside I tremble, but I have learned to put my trust in the Lord. I believe that is what Paul was stating in this passage.

Evidently, this lesson was one that Paul shared with the Corinthian church, as it had become puffed up and arrogant and focused on "talk":

> I am not writing this to shame you, but to warn you, as my dear children. Even though you have ten thousand guardians in Christ, you do not have many fathers, for in Christ Jesus I became your father through the gospel. Therefore I urge you to imitate me. For this reason I am sending to you Timothy, my son whom I love, who is faithful in the Lord. He will remind you of my way of life in Christ Jesus, which agrees with what I teach everywhere in every church.
>
> *Some of you have become arrogant,* as if I were not coming to you. But I will come to you very soon, if the Lord is willing, and then I will find out not only how these

arrogant people are talking, but what power they have. *For the kingdom of God is not a matter of talk but of power.*

1 Corinthians 4:14–20 (emphasis added)

If you recall from 1 Corinthians 2:5, Paul warned his readers not to put faith in the wisdom of men. He explained that their leaders had become arrogant in their knowledge, which resulted in pride. We, too, must be careful concerning this. Charisma is often mistaken for anointing. It is not an indication of truth; we must remain on guard. Personality is not power.

Paul knew their tendency to trust charisma, and so chose to not *wow* them with showmanship or knowledge. Because so many sermonizers had come on the scene, Paul felt the need to bring correction and instruction. Paul's message was that Christianity was not mere philosophy; it is all about a genuine relationship with a living God.

Paul's Humility and Power in God

Let's turn now to the segment of Paul's ministry when he was headed for Jerusalem and certain arrest. Even though disciples along the way pleaded with him not to go—for the Holy Spirit had revealed that chains awaited him—Paul remained steadfastly determined to preach where he believed the Lord had called him. Paul, willing to die for the sake of Christ, set his face like flint toward his destiny.

Paul was welcomed by the brethren when entering Jerusalem. When he went to the Temple, however, the Jews seized him. These Jews testified falsely, saying that Paul was teaching everyone everywhere against the people of

Israel and the Law and that "he has also [actually] brought Greeks into the temple; he has desecrated and polluted this holy place!" (Acts 21:28 AMPLIFIED). This alone would stir up the Jewish populace, for Gentiles were not allowed inside the holy Temple.

These false accusations turned the entire city of Jerusalem into an uproar; the people were thrown into great confusion. Dear one, let me mention that the enemy is always at the root of confusion. When you are confused, you can bet that the enemy has something destructive up his sleeve. In utter chaos, the people rushed together, grabbed Paul and dragged him outside the Temple, shutting the doors behind him.

The people were trying to kill him, beating him, when a commander of the Roman garrison took control with his troops. I can only imagine what was going through Paul's mind. Maybe he was thinking: *I used to do this to Christians!* Possibly, with every blow of someone's fist, Paul uttered a prayer of repentance for persecuting Christ and those who followed Him.

The Miraculous Testimony

The commander of the garrison in Jerusalem received word that the city was in an uproar, and went with soldiers to arrest Paul and secure him with chains. They took him to the barracks—the violent crowd still shouting for Paul's death—when something miraculous occurred: Paul convinced the commander to let him give his testimony to the crowd. Paul's testimony begins in Acts 22. I encourage you to grab your favorite Bible translation and read the entire passage.

Let me pull aside here and talk a little about *testimony*. Many people do not realize the power behind a testimony concerning God. Think of how the biblical stories were passed down through the generations, first orally, then written. These stories give testimony to the faithfulness of God. Every devout Jew was required to know the book of Deuteronomy inside-out for one simple reason: It is a very practical book. The instructions contained in Deuteronomy taught them about community life, work, relationships and worship. Even more, it made clear the people's obligation to "keep the commandments of the LORD your God, His *testimonies*, and His statutes which He has commanded" (Deuteronomy 6:17 NKJV, emphasis added).

Just what are testimonies of the Lord? The stories of God's love and His supernatural and covenant intervention in history. Testimonies are meant to be built upon. We are to remember continually what God has done and then declare it to the generations (see Deuteronomy 6:7).

I love what Bill Johnson writes in his insightful book *Release the Power of Jesus* (Destiny Image, 2009):

> When we declare the works of God we release a creative prophetic anointing that changes the atmosphere. In fact the declared testimony creates access for the very anointing that brought about the testimony in the first place—which was also released through a declaration—to bring it about again.

Johnson goes on to say: "This is the reality embedded in the very word *testimony*, 'to do it again.'"

When we give a *testimony* of what God has done, it creates an atmosphere and an anointing for someone to experience a testimony of his or her own. Today, for instance, when individuals give a testimony of being healed in a church service, they are declaring the goodness of God. Thus, they are encouraging a healing environment by saying, "God desires to do this again." How awesome!

Paul's Motive in Testimony

As Paul stood to give his public defense, he told the gathered throng the story of his life. Now, imagine Paul, bound with chains and defending himself—not with rational philosophy or brilliant oration or clever debate as he had done in Athens, but with a testimony. Yet there was much more to it: He was declaring and creating an atmosphere to change the hearts of the people. Repentance was available to an angry mob, and Paul desired to see it.

He confessed that he was a Jew who had studied at the feet of Gamaliel, was educated to give the strictest care to the Law and was a zealot for God—just like the crowd before him.

Then he confessed that he "harassed (troubled, molested, and persecuted) this Way [of the Lord] to the death, putting in chains and committing to prison both men and women" (Acts 22:4 AMPLIFIED). Paul acknowledged that he had persecuted Christians. And in verse 6 he begins the testimony that we know well—how he was on his way to Damascus when he had a *come-to-Jesus* meeting.

Let's heed the words of Paul's testimony and determine always to remain humble before the Lord. The ability to demonstrate the power of God will manifest when we allow Him to show us any limitations that stand in His way. If we struggle with feeling ineffective, He will shine His light in our hearts and teach us the power of testimony.

By the way, this was Paul's main message: He was blind and then saw the light. And not just in the natural. He truly saw the Light, Christ, his Savior and Redeemer.

Let's now pray for power.

Time for Reflection

1. Paul learned to press through, understanding that it was only God working through him that gave him the divine ability to overcome his limitations and express God's power on earth. Ask yourself if you withdraw when you feel persecuted. If you do, ask the Lord for grace to move past feeling that way. God desires to use you right where you are. You are His hands extended. Go ahead, pick up the phone and call someone and encourage him or her. You will be surprised how much better you feel as He empowers you to rise up above the limitation of feeling ineffective in your witness.

2. Maybe you have not had a preacher's "Blue Monday," but you have experienced some type of failure. Many times, especially if we are "works-oriented," we feel guilty and condemned when we have failed. Failure will lock us down quickly—almost paralyze us. Failure causes fear—fear of more failure. I would like for you to speak affirming words over yourself confirming your identity in Christ. This will get you up and moving forward once more. Remember this as you continue to journey with me. Do not try to have faith in *your* faith. Instead, have God's faith—the

faith of Him who lives in you. His faith will never let you down or condemn you.

3. Here are some affirming words to speak over yourself:

> I am a child of God (see 1 John 3:1).
> I am a new creation (see 2 Corinthians 5:17).
> I am a temple of the Holy Spirit (see 1 Corinthians 6:19).
> I am delivered from the domain of darkness into God's Kingdom (see Colossians 1:13).
> I am a saint, a holy one (see Romans 1:7; 1 Corinthians 1:2; Philippians 1:1; Ephesians 1:1).
> I am holy and without blame in His sight (see Ephesians 1:4; 1 Peter 1:16).
> I am brought near through the blood (see Ephesians 2:13).
> I am dead to sin and alive to God (see Romans 6:2, 11; 1 Peter 2:24).
> I am raised with Christ and seated in heavenly places (see Ephesians 2:6; Colossians 2:12).
> I have the mind of Christ (see 1 Corinthians 2:16).
> I have access to the Father through the Holy Spirit (see Ephesians 2:18; Hebrews 4:16).

Allow me to pray for you:

Father God, we come to You right now, to Your throne room, being allowed entrance due to the shed blood of Jesus Christ. We ask You to search our hearts. Open the eyes of our hearts that we might know You and know ourselves through Your eyes. We want to be a demonstration of Your power and glory. We desire to see heaven touch earth. Empower us to minister the Gospel with a pure heart and clean hands. We are thankful, Lord, that You have chosen each of us as Your own children, and that You have given us an inheritance through Christ. Teach us with Your wisdom. Let us not continue to lean to our own understanding, but completely trust in godly wisdom. In Jesus' name, Amen.

Precious one, there is so much more to learn. And it is so difficult for me not to begin to jump up and down as I know that you are being transformed as you continue to read. Let's continue our journey together.

4

A Dangerous Threefold Cord

Letting Go of Reliance on the Human Mind

Many of the ways God operates are paradoxical. Just think about it for a moment. We learn from the teachings of Jesus that the way up is down. To receive, we must first have a heart to give. To live we must die. He looks for the weak, the no-names, the foolish and despised. Then He inhabits them with His very own power and strength.

I want it to become obvious that demonstrating the Kingdom of God involves simple childlike faith rather than degrees and diplomas. We already have enough faith to step out and pray for others to be healed, delivered and restored. If you recall, God has given us *all* a measure of faith. But, unfortunately, we spend too much time asking for more and more and more faith—when we already have it.

Like Paul, we should rejoice in our weakness so that the power of Christ may rest upon us (see 2 Corinthians 12:9), but that does not mean that we need to see ourselves as weaklings—it is all about the attitude of the heart. When we become vulnerable, He is able to bring us to a place of restful dependence on a powerful God. Our vulnerability, in fact, is meant to release His presence into our lives. When we are vulnerable, we no longer trust our own wisdom, but rather align our thoughts with His thoughts. Since His ways are not our ways, why do we cling so often to our own intellect?

This leads us to a powerful limitation when it comes to demonstrating God's Kingdom and His power: "Greek thinking." As you continue to read, you will discover that humanism and intellectualism are connected to this kind of thinking. Like threads of a strong rope, the strands intertwine with another. Only by renewing our minds and having faith in God can we experience His power to transform the doubt and unbelief that seem too strong for us.

God is not against us using our minds—He gave us our minds for a reason. But His desire is to have our minds "renewed" so that nothing hinders us from walking in divine power and demonstration. In this chapter we focus on this threefold cord of *Greek thinking* and its close partners *humanism* and *intellectualism*. As we continue to discover, any reliance on the human mind severely limits our expression of the power of God.

And, precious believer, as we continue this journey, never lose sight of this important truth: God will always give you what Jesus deserved—His very best. Yes, God has His best planned for us. Allow confident expectation to arise. God is releasing divine tools for kingly living.

Threefold Cords

As you read, remember that the Word says that a threefold cord is not easily broken. I would like to refer to a specific quote from my book *Breaking the Threefold Demonic Cord: How to Discern and Defeat the Lies of Jezebel, Athaliah and Delilah* (Chosen, 2008). In that book I expose the evil seductions of a demonic threefold cord that is connected to a Jezebel spirit. I will discuss the spirit of Jezebel and her witchcrafts later in this book because witchcraft is activated by idol worship and intellectualism. For now, read what a threefold cord does and gain understanding of how Greek thinking, humanism and intellectualism can join as a team to hinder the supernatural.

As we pull down strongholds and demonic powers, we need to be aware of the threefold cord the enemy uses against us. Let's first examine the dynamics of a threefold cord.

The use of a triple braided cord, or rope, dates back thousands of years. Though ropes have been made of many different materials throughout the years, the most common rope used for its steadfast strength has been the triple braided cord. Modern technology has improved texture and durability, but in most circumstances a triple braided cord is still known for its tremendous strength. A rope with only two strands is not nearly as strong as a rope with three. The multiplication factor in the strength increases tremendously by the addition of one more cord. The strength of only two cords is unpredictable, but adding an additional cord proves almost invincible might.

The concept of a threefold cord takes on an entirely new dimension when considering it in the context of spiritual warfare. We must consider the use of the number three in our warfare against principalities and powers of darkness, Ecclesiastes 4:12 states, "Though one may be overpowered by another, two can withstand him. And a threefold cord is not quickly broken." In other words, if one person stands alone, he can be overpowered by another. Two can stand back-to-back and conquer. But when a third person joins the fight, the three have greater power and can overtake the oppressor, because a triple braided cord is not easily broken.

People hunger for the supernatural. And the more we hunger and thirst for God (as the Beatitudes suggest we are to do), the more we will hunger to see manifestations of the supernatural. This is all tied in to being completely satisfied:

> Blessed and fortunate and happy and spiritually prosperous (in that state in which the born-again child of God enjoys His favor and salvation) are those who hunger and thirst for righteousness (uprightness and right standing with God), for they shall be completely satisfied!
>
> Matthew 5:6 AMPLIFIED

Yet even as we hunger, there appears at the same time to be an increasing void of God's transforming power in most Christians' lives. The question is why. The first answer lies in intellectualism, Greek thinking and humanism. Just as legalism—*faith in achieving enough religious works*—will not cause God to accept or love us more, neither will these forms of thought—*faith in our head knowledge*—bring us any closer to God. To become completely satisfied in God is to experience our full inheritance, which includes witnessing and demonstrating the supernatural here on earth.

The second answer concerns our righteousness. We will discuss faith righteousness in a later chapter, but for now, consider the fact that our righteousness is not based upon human knowledge or religious works. Our righteousness is based solely upon the finished work of Christ at the cross.

Most of us have questions concerning the lack of power and demonstration of God in our lives, particularly since Jesus has given *us* all power and authority over the enemy. (The enemy is not merely a demon; I consider sickness and poverty also to be the enemy—among other things that rob us of our godly inheritance.) Let's study our potential for reliance on the human mind and the limitation it places upon us.

Greek Thinking and Intellectualism

Athens is the only city in the Bible referred to as one given over to idols. As we noted, the spiritual climate of Athens was described by Luke in Acts 17:16 as *kateidolo*, "wholly given to idolatry." And historians say that the city of Ephesus was so saturated with idols that it was difficult for traffic to progress through the streets. Each idol was carefully crafted by human hands, but was birthed in the minds of the craftsmen by Satan's evil overshadowing. Satan and his antichrist structures, including hierarchies of demonic authority, attempt to seduce individuals, families, governments and entire belief systems.

Idols were conceived in the heart of Satan when he desired to be worshiped. When Satan was cast out of heaven, he devised schemes that would affect generations of this world. This included his idols. If he had inspired an idol named "Satan," it would have been much too obvious. Instead he invaded the philosophies of mankind, the need for mankind to *know*.

It is my opinion that when Paul addressed the Greek philosophers in Athens, the demonic stronghold of intellect—including the territorial spirits assigned to Athens—affected him. As we have observed, even this strong disciple was unable to do much in that city. Though the Greek philosophers appeared interested in hearing the truth, when it was presented to them they responded with mental appraisals.

Paul exclaimed that they were too superstitious to hear the truth. He was aware of the demonic structure that had established itself and brainwashed the region. Paul, who delivered a powerful exhortation, was basically powerless to overthrow the demonic opposition there. Why? I believe that it is because he was focused on his oratory delivery. (What preacher or minister or evangelist or prophet has not been guilty of this at one time or another?) In other locales, Paul would preach and warlocks, occultists and witches would burn their fetishes and books of divination . . . just because he entered the city! Obviously he carried the *presence* of God with Him and, therefore, demonstrated His divine power.

But in the presence of a religious and legalistic spirit that drove him to *prove* himself worthy as an intellectual, Paul's ability to demonstrate God's power was dwarfed. This shows the insidiousness of this evil.

It is the same today when the Gospel is preached. All too often we seek those who are intellectual and sound good. They challenge our minds but never change our hearts, and because of this there is no demonstration of the power of God. God cannot prove Himself with man's head knowledge. He is Spirit and He manifests when His Spirit overrides human reasoning.

Too many people are caught up in their own thoughts to stop and discern the truth. Just as it was in ancient Athens, our Greek thinking keeps us from understanding—or wanting to understand—the resurrection. Just as in the time of Jesus and Paul, when truth is revealed, unclean spirits rise up and say "Leave us alone!" Dear one, this is the networking of a demonic system that seeks to infiltrate our belief systems. It is very apparent that the influence of ancient Greece is a stronghold in many societies today. In fact, in Western culture, we are influenced demonically by *a spirit of Greece* on a daily basis. Just as the apostles themselves witnessed the infiltration of Greek philosophy—loving wisdom—into the world around them, so are we defiled by this ungodly belief system.

Our Western culture has embraced intellectualism over divine revelation. Divine revelation is knowledge that God gives through our spirits. We receive this revelation by *spiritually* hearing, seeing and perceiving. Revelation allows us to understand something without having our natural senses activated. Put simply, revelation reveals what has been hidden. An example of this is when Peter received the revelation that Jesus was the Messiah only because the Father in heaven revealed it to him (see Matthew 16:17).

Natural Knowledge vs. Supernatural Knowledge

On Mars Hill the apostle Paul came toe to toe with philosophers. *Philosophy* is a science, a rational investigation that pursues wisdom. It is the love of wisdom as found through the intellect. This is predominately a type of wisdom birthed through a natural environment, void of God's revelation.

Paul spoke of the *wisdom of this age* when referring to Greek philosophy:

> We do, however, speak a message of wisdom among the mature, but not the wisdom of this age or of the rulers of this age, who are coming to nothing. No, we speak of God's secret wisdom, a wisdom that has been hidden and that God destined for our glory before time began. None of the rulers of this age understood it, for if they had, they would not have crucified the Lord of glory.
>
> 1 Corinthians 2:6–8

The Holy Spirit is the Teacher of wisdom and the Giver of divine revelation. He is the only source of God's wisdom or knowledge. Imagine the Holy Spirit hearing whatever is spoken in heaven and then teaching it to us on earth. What a visual!

Philosophers who rely on intellectualism cannot possibly operate in godly faith. Similarly, we, as believers, cannot rely on our head knowledge in order to walk in the supernatural. God is not understood through mere logic. Plato attempted to analyze God and came to the conclusion that God does not exist. Aristotle basically came to the same conclusion. Scientists have failed to categorize God because they do not understand that He is known and understood only by faith and divine revelation.

The key to operating in the supernatural is to activate our faith. Again, we already have a measure of faith—it is already in us. We will not be able to figure it out; we simply believe and do.

The natural realm directly opposes the spiritual realm. The natural realm is subject to time and space. It is expressed by dimensions that are accessed by our physical senses. The supernatural realm relies on neither time nor space. It remains in the invisible realm, yet it can be manifested in the natural through faith. In other words, what is invisible can be accessed and brought into the natural by faith. Whatever is unseen can be made manifest in the natural by speaking God's Word and activating our faith.

It is time to access the unseen.

Why Not Miracles?

Dear one, I have been attempting to give you a *charge* as you read. I am praying as I write that your faith, much like being plugged in to an electrical outlet, is receiving current for experiencing God's power.

I trust you realize by now that Greek thinking and intellectualism hinder the supernatural. Miracles involve the supernatural—and the natural opposes the supernatural. I define a miracle as "the supernatural intervention of God that invades the natural realm." All through Scripture are instances where God interrupts what is happening in natural time or space. We read in Joshua 10:12–13 that Joshua commanded, "'O sun, stand still over Gibeon, O moon, over the Valley of Aijalon.' So the sun stood still, and the moon stopped, till the nation avenged itself on its enemies."

God can stop time whenever He desires. I have experienced what is known as an open vision. In one particular vision, I was in a battle against the kingdom of darkness. The battle raged for what seemed like hours; yet upon being quickened back to natural time it seemed as though no time had been lost at all. God loves to get us to think "outside the box." I believe it is safe to say that the supernatural is "outside the box"—how about you? We may as well admit it: We cannot box God into the confines of our understanding, and, if we try, He will always prove us wrong. Nothing can limit God, so why do we try?

Limiting God hinders the miraculous. The Bible records many miracles performed by God. I will list only a few; please, do your own biblical study. You will be so blessed when you do.

1. God destroyed Sodom and Gomorrah with fire from heaven (see Genesis 19:24–25).
2. He brought Isaac forth from an old man (Abraham) and his sterile wife (see Genesis 21:1–3).
3. God spoke to Moses from a burning bush—a bush that was unconsumed with fire (see Exodus 3).
4. God parted the Red Sea as He delivered Israel from Egyptian slavery (see Exodus 13:17–14:30).
5. He destroyed the walls of Jericho with a shout from His people (see Joshua 6).
6. He caused an animal—a donkey—to speak (see Numbers 22).
7. He used Elijah to command a leper, Naaman, to dip in the Jordan, and healed him as he dipped the seventh time (see 2 Kings 5:1–14).
8. He preserved Shadrach, Meshach and Abednego from a fiery furnace (see Daniel 3).

9. He closed the mouth of a lion when Daniel was thrown into the lions' den (see Daniel 6:10–23).

Look at the miracles Jesus, God's Son, performed. Here are a few examples:

1. He healed a centurion's servant (see Matthew 8:5–13).
2. He cursed a fig tree, causing it to dry up (see Matthew 21:18–22).
3. He multiplied bread and fish, feeding five thousand people (see Mark 6:30–44).
4. He restored sight to a blind beggar (see Mark 10:46–52).
5. He healed ten lepers (see Luke 17:11–19).
6. He turned water into wine (see John 2:1–11).
7. He raised Lazarus from the dead (see John 11:38–44).

Yet, precious believer, the greatest miracle of all is our salvation. To become "born again" means that we no longer are subject to a sinful nature, but can become filled with the Spirit of God. This is because Jesus surrendered to the cross and shed His blood for the remission of our sins. Jesus took the keys of death from Satan and was raised from the dead. As He ascended to heaven, the Holy Spirit was sent to empower us to do the same signs, wonders and miracles as Jesus did.

Humanism

Now let's talk about humanism—and, yes, notice the word *human*. That says enough right there, does it not?

Humanism is a study, philosophy, worldview or practice that focuses on *human* values and concerns. Humanism exalts *human* nature above God and the supernatural. Bottom line—man is exalted above God, and man's ideas above God's wisdom. In its purest form humanism positions man essentially as a god. Humanism got a boost during the Renaissance period, which began around the fourteenth century, when the Greek ideals of thought and reason were once again revered. This was reflected in philosophy, the arts and even religion.

Since humanism elevates the wisdom of man, it directly opposes *godly* wisdom. We are instructed in the Bible to seek God and not make decisions without Him. We face pressure daily to make decisions—but we must never leave God out of the equation. The disciples learned this. Not until the Holy Spirit came were they truly able to apply the principles taught by Jesus.

It is the will of God to give us His divine wisdom. Our reliance on humanism limits this process. How? God loves it when we dream with Him. He desires to download His wisdom to spark our creativity. Whether we are artists, musicians, builders, homemakers, educators or merchants, God wants to release His creativity to us. But if we think we know better, or never even stop to ask God for His input, we effectively shut down the ability to receive His supernatural power.

Humanism causes our dreams to be independent of God. But our dreams should exist *because* of God. When I fully realized that God wanted to release His wisdom so that I could become more creative, it took me to a whole new level in my writing. Wisdom and creativity are related subjects biblically. Consider that the "first mention" of a person filled with the Holy Spirit was Bezalel. This man needed the wisdom of God as he headed up Moses' building project. Moses was commissioned by God to build Him a tabernacle in the desert—this is where Bezalel came into the picture. God gave him supernatural wisdom to get the job done with an artistic spirit of excellence (see Exodus 31:2–5).

Now, think about this. What if this craftsman had decided he could do it a different way—maybe take a shortcut or two? That would touch upon humanism, right?

I know that is a simple illustration, but it is a clear example of how we can easily exalt ourselves above God. Not heeding God's directions says, "I know a better way," and that, my friend, is humanism.

A carnal mind is based upon this world's reality and is basically anti-God. Now be sure not to misunderstand me. We need intelligence, but we need to couple it with godly wisdom. If you recall, Solomon asked for wisdom above riches; God gave him wisdom *and* riches. The Queen of Sheba visited the king and was in awe of his wisdom. This is because he was blessed with "godly wisdom" and was not reliant on limited human creativity.

The Body of Christ seems presently to be short-circuiting God as to what is "normal" and operating mainly on human ability. If everything has to be reasoned or understood, there is no room for the Holy Spirit to manifest through miracles. Miracles are not of the natural—but the supernatural. As such, miracles should be part of a *normal* church service or the result of *normal* prayer.

Since I have been writing this book, the miracles that I witnessed have increased. It is becoming a *normal* manifestation that whenever I pray for the sick many are supernaturally healed. Whenever I suggest others in the congregation pray for each other, it is now becoming more *normal* for frozen shoulders to be healed, legs to grow, joints to be healed, scoliosis to disappear and backs to be straightened. It is becoming more *normal* for pain to leave bodies. Believer, when God says to pray for the sick and they shall recover—He means it.

Humanism has robbed the Church of faith and expectancy for the supernatural. Now, expect to witness the miraculous so that we can continue to give God glory through our testimonies. Remember, a testimony means "Do it again, God!"

Time for Reflection

Take a few moments and reflect on God and what He has done for you. This is a time to be thankful. Remaining thankful opens the heavens for miracles to occur. Write below what you are thankful for:

1. I am thankful for _____.
2. I am thankful for _____.
3. I am thankful for _____.
4. I am thankful for _____.
5. I am thankful for _____.

Did you struggle to thank God for just five things? If you did, it is possible that you have cluttered your mind with problems that appear bigger than God. Take a few moments and imagine just how *big* God is. Problems and strongholds are dwarfed in His presence. Precious one, His presence is with you right now. The Holy Spirit lives in you—His Temple. Take a few more minutes and write down a few more areas for which you are thankful.

Now, stand up and declare the specifics for which you are thankful. You might even call a friend or prayer partner and confess the goodness of God. As you do this, you are releasing a testimony. As you give testimony, you let go of your limitations and create an atmosphere for the miraculous to occur. Try always to remember that when a testimony is given, that testimony makes the atmosphere pregnant for another testimony to manifest. Now how easy is that to experience the supernatural? Go for it!

Give Him all the glory for the great things He has done.

Oneness with God positions you with authority over the enemy.

Faith in God moves mountains.

Our relationship with God is more important than religion.

Rest in His divine ability to give you wisdom when needed.

Intellegence void of God's wisdom positions us for failure rather than victory.

The way to get God's attention is to admit how much we need Him.

5

Legalism vs. Faith Righteousness

Letting Go of a Faulty Foundation

It was one of those days when nothing seemed to go right. I feel certain that you have had one of those. This is how it went: The computer crashed, the cell phone went dead in the midst of an important radio interview, I lost the car keys and our air conditioner broke (we live in Texas). On top of that . . . it was "a bad hair day." That affected me the most; there is just no humility for that challenge.

At the end of the day, I was a little calmer as I was able to locate my car keys and drive around in air conditioning. I noticed the gasoline gauge was low so I whipped into the nearest place to gas up. While filling up, I heard the loud voice of someone who was cursing and glanced over to see—I mean, this was really bad cursing. My frayed-nerve impulse was to shout back at the young man to please keep his opinions to himself, but I held my tongue. Then,

I noticed him walking into the convenience store, and his pants were hanging down so low that there was more exposure than I wanted to see.

Suddenly I had had it. My temper at that point could have made a mercury thermometer have a complete blowout. I decided independently that it was *my* responsibility to set this young man straight—tell him a few things; you know, a few *religious adjustments*. Maybe you can relate to this fact: *For some ungodly reason we, as believers, feel that we are responsible to fix others.* I now realize that this attitude stems from the sin of judging others.

When I walked into the store behind him, the Holy Spirit said to me, *Sandie, the way to show My glory here is to love this young man and pray for him.* Then He reminded me of the Scripture that says it is the goodness of God that leads to repentance. But I tossed godly wisdom to the side. I simply could not shake my anger toward this young man. At least I kept silent, and turned around and walked back to my car and sat inside for a while trying to identify the root of my attitude.

I am not so easily provoked; what made me want to lash out in hatred toward a child whom God loves? Yes, God is love and He loves that young man just as much as He loves me. I realized, for the first time, *really* realized, that I had become judgmental toward others. Not only that, God opened the eyes of my heart and I saw something very disturbing. Jesus said that if we are angry we are "in danger of the fire of hell" (Matthew 5:22), and John wrote that whoever "hates his brother is a murderer, and you know that no murderer has eternal life abiding in him" (see 1 John 3:15). Now I did not murder this young man, but since I had judged him in my *heart*, it was the same as the sin of murder. When we judge others, we have assumed a responsibility that belongs solely to God.

Relying on Our Own Strength

Legalism, as we have learned, is an attempt, through our human effort, to please God in our own strength. It is any attempt to become holy or righteous through religious works, rules or traditions. Legalism ignores the finished work at the cross. God asks that we simply "believe" the fact that we are justified by our faith in Jesus and His finished work at the cross. Christ has redeemed us from the curse of the Law because He went to the cross and became that curse for us (see Galatians 3:13).

Legalism requires strict adherence to the Law or a doctrine. When we are yoked with legalism, there will always be a religious spirit at our side. A *religious spirit* functions like this: It is a lying spirit that says that we have to act religious in order to please God. Perhaps we believe that we must pray for two hours to get God's attention, or never miss a church service, or witness to the lost out of Christian duty rather than passion. And, if we do not do everything perfectly, we give way to condemnation. Or we get so busy quoting Scriptures aloud, feeling this somehow impresses God, that we miss His invitation simply to meditate on His Word and be still in His presence.

Legalism hinders the move of God in our lives. The Holy Spirit gently leads but a religious spirit *drives* us and never satisfies. Legalism digs a deep pit of chronic dissatisfaction because we are more concerned about our religion than our relationship with God. Now please note: I am not suggesting that using our faith to declare God's Word with expectation is legalism. There is a godly balance to all of this. My main concern is that, even in our obedience to speak His Word in faith, we also rely on His grace to guide us. His divine grace is what empowers us to fulfill our divinely given commission on earth. To think we can do this in our own strength is where legalism takes root.

I hate to admit I have firsthand experience with legalism. The day I saw what was in my heart—that I had judged that young man because of how he acted and looked—I realized that I was judgmental and legalistic. Let me be honest: The legalism had been there for a long time, but this was the first time I saw it in my heart. (I was prepared to "adjust" this young man and explain how disappointing he was to God. How dare I?)

Legalism toward others evolves in many ways. If others worship differently, we suspect them. If they adhere to different doctrines, we judge them as unholy or not as "religious" as ourselves—thus revealing a heart condition that is unhealthy and unpleasing to God. On the other hand, there is a difference between judging and discerning. One can discern that someone needs Christ and pray for guidance as to how to lead that one to Him, but judgment takes an entirely different avenue—it puts us in the judgment seat and only Christ belongs there.

We are justified solely by the blood of Jesus. This is made clear in Romans 5:8–9:

> God demonstrates his own love for us in this: While we were still sinners, Christ died for us. Since we have now

been justified by his blood, how much more shall we be saved from God's wrath through him!

Notice again, the key phrase is *justified by his blood.* *Justify* and *justification* are key words in the New Testament. To *justify* means "to make righteous, to acquit from sin and to hold guiltless." Scripture is clear that we are only righteous because of His blood—not a list of rules or laws. When we receive Christ as our Savior we are, thereby, justified. And what is more, we receive the righteousness of Jesus Christ—not our own righteousness.

Faith Is Witnessing the Impossible

Most of us as "people of faith" cut our teeth on Hebrews 11:1, which says "Now faith is the substance of things hoped for, the evidence of things not seen" (KJV). This passage is foundational for breaking through our limitations and believing God for the supernatural. Without a foundation, nothing can stand. So, when we observe this passage as foundational, we realize that if any part of this passage is not fully understood, then our faith might falter. In other words, if a foundation cracks or breaks, the walls will then shift, doors will not close properly, etc. We must, therefore, understand the full revelation of this passage to bring the unseen realm into the seen realm.

Unfortunately, most of us have been taught for years that if we just pray enough (doing something ourselves) we can "fake it until we make it." But we are like someone building on a faulty foundation. The real reason we are not seeing positive results when we pray in faith is that we do not truly believe in our hearts that God desires His best for us.

The words *substance of things hoped for* mean that we should have confident expectation. Pessimistic-minded believers cannot seem to grasp this truth and seldom see positive results when they pray. It is possible, however, for anyone to break free from negativity if the mind is renewed. (We discuss renewing the mind several times throughout this book.) You have to admit: Pessimism is a form of faith; it is, however, faith that destroys.

As we have confident expectation, God allows us to see the evidence of what we pray for. He releases His power, making it active in our lives, so that we witness what is not seen. In other words, what seemed impossible becomes possible.

Hebrews 11:3 states that by faith (immovable trust) "we understand that the worlds were framed by the word of God"; therefore, we, as sons and daughters of God, can speak forth into our lives the provisions that God has made for us. This is important to realize as we learn more about experiencing God's transforming power: We can "frame our world" by speaking the Word of God. In other words, something tangible comes from something invisible. If, however, it is not settled in our hearts how much God loves us and desires His best for us, we will limit the results.

All too often we try to move forth in the miraculous by believing we have to get enough faith to "get God to do something." But, dear one, we already have everything we need—the potential to access the unseen through our words and our beliefs. We are not attempting to create something from nothing; we are attempting to believe that

God is pleased with our faith and longs to provide what we are believing for. Let's read what Jesus said about faith in Mark 11:22–23:

> "Have faith in God," Jesus answered. "I tell you the truth, if anyone says to this mountain, 'Go, throw yourself into the sea,' and does not doubt in his heart but believes that what he says will happen, it will be done for him."

Jesus makes it clear that we must believe "in our hearts" and never be distracted—never doubting, believing to the end. It is important to maintain the soil of our hearts and not allow it to become hardened due to the cares of life.

But let me add something very important. Faith cannot be conjured up. It is pointless to try and try to stir up more and more faith. We all have a measure of faith already. And beyond that, faith comes from love. The more we love the Father, the stronger our faith becomes. The key, then, is to draw near to Him daily so that your faith will become fresh for whatever it is you might need it for. It is God's responsibility to do the miracle; we are just the vessels who pray, seek God and ask for the miracle. Knowing that He loves us—and the person we might be burdened to pray for—empowers us with more faith to access the unseen. Our responsibility is to keep the garden of our hearts rid of thorns and thistles so that we can reap a harvest of miracles.

Faith Righteousness

Now that we understand that faith is needed if we are to experience the kind of power that transforms, let me bump this subject up a notch and say this: It is not because you are doing anything "right" in your own power—*even the fact of exercising faith*—that releases the miracles. Many people believe that because they have faith God will honor them with demonstrations of His power. The truth is this: It is solely through Jesus' sacrifice that we became the righteousness of God. It was not our own righteousness or any kind of human righteousness, but the very righteousness of God Himself.

We must, however, have *faith* to receive it. This is why I use the term *faith righteousness*. The accuser will lie to believers and remind us of our failures. He will attempt to deceive us into thinking that we have fallen from grace and are now *unrighteous* because we have sinned. The Word says, however, that there is no more condemnation for those who are in Christ. When believers sin, we are not condemned—we are still loved and God still considers us righteous based on the finished work of Christ. We stand on that foundation of faith in our righteousness through Christ. Now, when we fall into sin, of course, we need to repent before God, but we repent knowing that we are forgiven because Christ shed His blood for that sin. Bottom line, the Word says that "these signs [miracles] will accompany those who believe" (Mark 16:17). All we have to do is be willing to be used—keeping our eyes on Jesus, not the strength of our willingness—and the signs follow.

It is important always to remember that Christ died to make you righteous. You do not lose righteousness when you sin, and God does not love you any less. If you sin, repent and let your *faith righteousness* empower you.

I am often amazed at how people respond to the word *repent*. I watch some cower down as if God were ready to smack them because they have done something wrong. But, actually, the word *repent* means "to change the way we think." Both the Old and New Testaments describe repentance as being "sorry" for our wrong actions and turning from them. We need to be "sorry," but not to be overwhelmed with condemnation due to the sin. Again, there is no condemnation in Christ. When the Holy Spirit spoke to my heart that day at the gas station, I felt instantly sorrowful for my actions—but more was needed from me. I needed to change the way I thought: I needed to see that young man as God saw Him.

In other words, I needed to repent and change the way I was looking at him. (There was much more that I needed to work on, but that was at the top of the list for the moment.) My responsibility was not to condemn myself for my judgmental attitude, but to see myself as a new creation and to see this young man as a creation of Christ also.

To walk in the supernatural is to be led by the Holy Spirit.

Prideful Attitudes

You see, Christians often believe we are better than others and that we have more favor with God because we *do* more for Him. This attitude is prideful, and its faulty foundation hinders many from receiving salvation. My friend, we can do absolutely nothing to cause God to love us more than He already does. And He loves the sinners as much as the saints. But when discussing our righteousness we need not ever to forget this fact: *When we receive Jesus as our Savior, we are immediately made righteous.* It is the shed blood of Jesus that makes us righteous—*not what we do for God.*

I was legalistic, judgmental and "religious." Yes, I see it so clearly now. In fact, maybe it was one of those "mysteries" God speaks of in Scripture—especially when Jesus said there is more to tell us, but we cannot always, at the time, bear the weightiness of the revelation attached to it. Laugh with me, please; I do not know if I could have admitted that I had a religious spirit until now.

None of this (legalism, being judgmental and acting religious) is pleasing to the Lord. When I realized the fact that I felt *more righteous* than others simply because I serve the Lord in a different capacity, I had to repent for my pride and pious attitude. After all, I really worked *hard* at being righteous! I was misunderstanding the truth that we can be saved only because Christ laid down His life at the cross. The price for sin was paid by the shed blood of Jesus.

Most of us, when we became born again (giving our lives to God), were never taught that we were instantly righteous in God's eyes. Instead, we are given a list of rules (spoken or unspoken) so that we can try harder to stay in God's favor. If we will begin to see ourselves as righteous in Christ, we will experience supernatural grace that is released to live a godly life.

Now, faith must be active in order to continue to see ourselves as righteous. The accuser of the brethren is constantly lying to us concerning our identity in Christ. I want to discuss more on God's grace later, but it is important for us to realize that God desires to open our eyes to His truths concerning righteousness. When Jesus came to heal the blind eyes, He dealt with more than literal blindness; He also confronted spiritual blindness. Unless we are serving God with a pure heart—out of love—all of our efforts are simply wood, hay and stubble that will burn in the holy fire of God.

Read below how we must build solely on the foundation of Jesus Christ (and His righteousness):

> For other foundation can no man lay than that is laid, which is Jesus Christ. Now if any man build upon this foundation gold, silver, precious stones, wood, hay, stubble; every man's work shall be made manifest: for the day shall declare it, because it shall be revealed by fire; and the fire shall try every man's work of what sort it is.
>
> 1 Corinthians 3:11–13 KJV

When Jesus went to the cross and shed His blood, He loosed the supernatural grace of God. Grace is described as unmerited favor or an undeserved gift. Because of His eternal presence with us, He imparts through grace His supernatural power that gives us a divine ability to do things we cannot accomplish in our own strength. When we attempt to do things for God in our own strength, we become even more legalistic. This is what happened to the Galatians. Paul addressed them saying that they were foolish because they started out with complete dependence upon the Holy Spirit but now they were performing in the flesh:

> You foolish Galatians! Who has *bewitched* you? Before your very eyes Jesus Christ was clearly portrayed as crucified. I would like to learn just one thing from you: Did you receive the Spirit by observing the law, or by believing what you heard? Are you so foolish? After beginning

with the Spirit, are you now trying to attain your goal by human effort?

Galatians 3:1–3 (emphasis added)

Being Bewitched

Did you notice the italicized word *bewitched* in this passage? Paul was pointing out that Satan was attempting to counteract the finished work of the cross with a *spirit of witchcraft*.

The Galatians had started out in the Spirit, as they were saved, filled with the Spirit and continually witnessed the miraculous. But now witchcraft had influenced them to follow unbiblical rules and norms, and they had given in to carnality. All of this caused them to lose sight of God's supernatural power.

A study of the word *bewitched* can give us a clear picture of how the enemy desires for us to feel that we can take credit for our righteousness. In fact, the message of our being righteous *only* because of the blood and *not* because of what we do was the very stumbling block over which the Pharisees tripped.

Being bewitched refers to "being out of one's mind, astonished or overwhelmed with wonder." Another use of being bewitched means to "fascinate by false representation." It is closely linked to *divination* and *sorcery*. It is safe to say that *legalism opens the door to the occult*. The occult attempts to keep truth hidden, and revelation brings truth into the light. The Holy Spirit is revealing mysteries in this season; is it any wonder that Satan will attempt to keep us in darkness by thinking so well of ourselves? The apostle Paul was concerned that the Galatians had been led to accept a teaching contrary to the Gospel of Christ. And, using the word *bewitched* points to an occult source through which evil forces were effectively at work.

I find it interesting that a more thorough study of *bewitched* leads to the concept of an exalted opinion of someone—or oneself—due to a "fascination" regarding "professions." This causes me to think it possible that someone with eloquent speech had fascinated the Galatians, and, therefore, their eyes were no longer on Christ but on the minister. Ouch! Been there, done that. How about you? I feel safe to say that we have all at one time or another been fascinated by a charismatic personality. But let me ask: *Was there evidence of God's transforming power?*

Charismatic Ministers

Now I suppose that this a good time to talk about the character and fruit of a minister. Sadly, we have witnessed many ministers who were charismatically appealing and who experienced the miraculous manifesting in their ministries but who fell into immorality. I know that this is misleading and disappointing to everyone—including the unchurched. The Word states that gifts and calling of God are irrevocable or "without repentance" (Romans 11:29 KJV), so God often does not remove the anointing from someone's life—even though that one might be unrepentant about sin.

Once again, we cannot judge—but we can discern the character of the minister and use wisdom about that minister's teaching. I recall one time when an individual was ministering in miracles, but my "spiritual discernment alarm" sounded loudly. People were genuinely healed, and yet the minister was later exposed for immorality. We must leave the judgment part to God, but heed our discernment—the Holy Spirit's quickening of our hearts and minds—in times like these. God desires to heal. Let's determine that we will be holy vessels in which He can demonstrate power. Believe me, just taking care of *me* and my personal relationship with God is a full-time job. I do not have time to look for faults in others!

If the gifting is present, it is possible to have a charismatic (in the sense of popular and well-received) ministry with enough effort—and with very little reliance on the Holy Spirit. It seems likely that the Galatians were so caught up in religious works they felt haughty and prideful—as if *they* had received a greater level of righteousness—without needing Christ. Dear one, let's have *faith righteousness*. It gives us a firm foundation and enables us to walk in the grace of God and His supernatural power.

Human Theology and Ability

Theology is a systematic and rational study of the nature of God and religion. It is, however, mere study. In other words, there is not necessarily any supernatural power connected to what is learned because it involves the human mind and reasoning. Revelation is needed for the supernatural power of God to flow. The proper way to use study to help us become effective for the Kingdom is to ask the Lord for divine revelation. Studying is very important—again, the key here is balance. Studying the Word of God and combining it with the teaching and revelation of the Holy Spirit is what will transform our lives. The Holy Spirit is our Teacher; however, that does not negate our need to be accountable to a pastor, elder or mentor who is mature spiritually.

Dear one, it is when we put confidence in our own abilities, our own strength and our own intellectual acumen that we separate ourselves from the Spirit of God. This is an example of how we come to depend more on "religion" than the Holy Spirit. If you have fallen into this, take heart. It does not mean that you were never saved or born again. No, if you are aware of falling in this area, the Lord wants to renew your mind as to your righteousness in Christ. Actually, this should relieve you of all the stress of religious works and religious activity that piles on with religious condemnation.

If we handle divine situations with our carnal minds, we will always limit God. We cannot operate in the supernatural with our carnal minds. This is why the mind must be renewed. It is faith that gives us the ability to rise above human reasoning. I am sure that you can think of many people in the Bible who did things that made absolutely no sense to them. Yet, the supernatural occurred whenever they obeyed the Spirit. Moses was one of those people. God told him to stretch out his rod, and the Red Sea parted. He used a stick to strike a rock for water to come forth and refresh millions of people. The Israelites shouted down a wall at Jericho. Jesus made a mudpack to heal eyes . . . it goes on and on. It should be going on for us, too.

Grace and Traditions of Men

I know I touched on this earlier also, but I want to mention it again. Grace is the divine ability given to us by God to become everything He has called us to be. We, in the natural, would be unable to accomplish these things in our own strength; our human ability will attempt to replace God's grace. To move in the supernatural requires complete dependence upon the grace of God. It is His power flowing through us—it is *not* our own efforts that create an atmosphere for the miraculous.

Nor will the traditions of man have an effect when we desire the supernatural. Mark 7:13 says, "[You make] the word of God of no effect through your tradition which you have handed down" (NKJV). It is true. There are certain church traditions that have been passed down from generation to generation. Sadly, many leaders lean more on tradition than the Word. These leaders are nullifying the Word and power of God. A tradition is not always from God. If the tradition is not producing life transformation, it needs a careful consideration for removal. Traditions are never meant to replace a move of God's Spirit or become a substitute for the Word of God.

If we took a close look at many of the Church's traditions, it might explain why many are not witnessing the supernatural. There is a lack of power in the Church because many have become performance-based ministers. The teaching has become more "entertaining" than revelatory; the preaching is more "charismatic" than anointed.

Grieving and Quenching the Spirit

In Greek, the word for *grieve* is *lypeo*, which means "to make sorrowful, to affect with sadness, to cause grief, to throw into sorrow, to offend." How do we offend God or grieve Him? The following passage makes it clear—we are to live a godly lifestyle. If we have evil attitudes, slanderous conversations and bitter quarrels, then we impede the Spirit from flowing through us. But consider also the pride of self-righteousness—it completely limits our access to the power of the blood. Yes, a judgmental attitude will grieve the Spirit of God and affect our ability to walk in the supernatural power of God.

> And do not *grieve* the Holy Spirit of God, with whom you were sealed for the day of redemption. Get rid of all bitterness, rage and anger, brawling and slander, along with every form of malice. Be kind and compassionate to one another, forgiving each other, just as in Christ God forgave you.
>
> Ephesians 4:30–32 (emphasis added)

In Greek, the word *quench* is *sbennymi*, meaning "to extinguish things on fire, to suppress, stifle." The New International Version says, "Do not put out the Spirit's fire."

> *Quench not* the Spirit. Despise not prophesyings. Prove all things; hold fast that which is good. Abstain from all appearance of evil. And the very God of peace *sanctify* you wholly; and I pray God your whole spirit and soul and body be preserved blameless unto the coming of our Lord Jesus Christ.
>
> 1 Thessalonians 5:19–23 KJV (emphasis added)

Notice that we are to keep the flames burning by abstaining from evil. Dear one, we cannot do this in our own strength—there must be complete dependence on His divine grace. Did you notice that when we are experiencing the fire of God that the God of peace *sanctifies* us wholly? That word *sanctify* is connected to the provision of the blood. Yes, the blood of Jesus sanctifies us. *Sanctification* means "to make holy" and "to set apart."

Dear one, we are standing on a faulty foundation if we take credit for holiness; we are holy only due to the blood. We cannot work up holiness, pray long hours to become more holy—we are already made holy when we receive Christ as Savior. To believe that what we do for God makes us holy is a form of legalism—working our way to heaven through deeds rather than relationship.

Hebrews 13:12 says, *"Therefore Jesus also, that He might sanctify the people with His own blood, suffered outside the gate"* (NKJV, emphasis added). In other words, He was crucified outside of the city as He sanctified the people through His very own blood.

Precious one, I am hungering to experience God's power. I know you are too. In the next chapter we will explore more closely our position in Christ, and the mandate we have to exhibit His power.

Time for Reflection

1. Our lives are filled with the consequences of our words. When we judge others, our hearts speak with words that condemn. Ask the Holy Spirit if you need to repent of being judgmental toward someone. If you do, repent. Remember not to feel condemned, but rather to recognize the fact that you are redeemed by Jesus and, by grace, receive His righteousness. See yourself as He sees you. Confess that you are righteous through Christ Jesus. Then pray for the person you have judged and confess something positive over his or

her life. Nullify the false judgment by your confession and repentance. Remember life and death are in the power of the tongue—speak life. Your prayer might be something similar to this:

> *Lord, I repent for the judgment I made against my brother or sister. I realize both that You love all mankind and that I do not have the authority to judge. I nullify any words that I spoke in judgment, and I break off any demonic activity loosed against someone because of my words. I also desire to forgive those who have misjudged me. In Jesus' name, Amen.*

2. As you read this chapter, did the Holy Spirit bring to your mind an incident where you really felt good about something "religious" you performed? If so, can you take that action to the throne right now and talk to the Lord about it? A simple conversation like this is just a suggestion:

> *Lord,* [confess here, such as:] *I stayed later than everyone else at the altar that day in order to look more religious and dedicated to prayer. I realize now that I am righteous only because of the cross of Christ. Forgive me for drawing attention to myself. I submit to the Holy Spirit to impress upon my heart any time I am choosing to stand on a faulty foundation.*

3. Have you been like me and ever felt "driven"? Now you know that it is linked to legalism. Take some time and

think back over your life. When did you feel driven? Once you can identify an incident, take it to God and talk to Him about it. Ask the Lord for the root cause behind being driven. Sometimes, for instance, when people are born poor they are driven to be rich no matter the cost. This is a good time to repent, turn from that behavior and change the way you think.

Precious believer, we can come before the Lord with confidence. Below is a prayer you might want to pray to confirm your position in Jesus.

> *Through the blood of Jesus, I am sanctified, made holy, set apart to God. I do not have to work hard in my own strength. The Bible says to be holy, just as the Lord is holy. I affirm, therefore, that I am holy and righteous because of the blood of Jesus. The devil has no place in me. I renounce any area of the occult that has been affecting me due to my feeling that I am responsible for my own righteousness. I am healed and delivered and sanctified through the blood of Jesus. Today, I possess faith knowing that I am holy and righteous and, therefore, empowered to walk in the supernatural. I choose to stand on a firm foundation. I am free because Christ has set me free! Amen.*

6

Who, Exactly, Are You?

Letting Go of Bondage

Imagine yourself being used mightily by God. Mark 16:17–18 (KJV) describes our divine commissioning.

> And these signs shall follow them that believe; in my name shall they cast out devils; they shall speak with new tongues; they shall take up serpents; and if they drink any deadly thing, it shall not hurt them; they shall lay hands on the sick, and they shall recover.

This is a commissioning that is achieved only by "believing," and the power comes simply by "doing." As we learned in the last chapter, through the finished work of Christ this power comes through faith and not human striving. Is that not wonderful news? When we "believe," we are not believing in order to access His power; rather, we are empowered with faith because of who we are in Christ.

We need to remind ourselves that we do not have the power—He does. We are simply the obedient ones, empowered by divine grace, to do His will on earth. And any misunderstanding of the power of the finished work of Jesus at the cross, of our inheritance through Him and of just who we are in Christ will dwarf our usefulness to do His signs and wonders.

Paul described who we are in Christ. Let's take a closer look:

> Therefore, brothers, we have an obligation—but it is not to the sinful nature, to live according to it. For if you live according to the sinful nature, you will die; but if by the Spirit you put to death the misdeeds of the body, you will live, because those who are led by the Spirit of God are sons of God. For you did not receive a spirit that makes you a slave again to fear, but you received the Spirit of sonship. And by him we cry, "Abba, Father." The Spirit himself testifies with our spirit that we are God's children. Now if we are children, then we are heirs—heirs of God and co-heirs with Christ, if indeed we share in his sufferings in order that we may also share in his glory.
>
> Romans 8:12–17

Precious saint, it is time that we begin to manifest as sons and daughters of God. We are no longer slaves. We will *never* walk in the full demonstration of power until we see ourselves as those who receive an inheritance through Christ. When the apostle Paul said that we are no longer slaves, but rather bondservants of Christ (see 1 Corinthians 7:21–23), he was referring to the option slaves were given, once set free, to choose to remain with their masters. By doing so, they became bondservants, serving out of devotion rather than obligation. In essence, when we choose to become servants, that is where the power kicks in. We demonstrate the will of the King as His ambassadors, and are empowered with signs, wonders and miracles—all evident because we "believe" who we are in Christ.

Some people think that Jesus came just to give us another set of "rules." After all, even though we are no longer under the Law, there are still divine directives given in the New Testament. This is one of the reasons that many hold on to a "works mentality." They miss the point that God's laws and teachings are meant to be written on the tablets of our hearts; no longer must we adhere to laws written on tablets of stone. Not only does God's grace save us and empower us to do His will, but *God's grace helps us remain obedient while serving Him.*

I love to read Romans 8 as it declares the power and goodness of God. Here are a few liberating verses concerning our royal lineage and God's grace toward us who believe in Him:

> The Spirit himself testifies with our spirit that we are God's children. Now if we are children, then we are *heirs—heirs of God and co-heirs with Christ,* if indeed we share in his sufferings in order that we may also share in his glory. I consider that our present sufferings are not worth comparing with the glory that will be revealed in us. The creation waits in *eager expectation for the sons of God to be revealed.*
>
> For the creation was subjected to frustration, not by its own choice, but by the will of the one who subjected it,

in hope that the creation itself will be liberated from its bondage to decay and brought into the glorious freedom of the children of God.

We know that the whole creation has been *groaning as in the pains of childbirth* right up to the present time. Not only so, but we ourselves, who have the first fruits of the Spirit, groan inwardly as we wait eagerly for our adoption as sons, the redemption of our bodies.

Romans 8:16–23 (emphasis added)

In these verses we notice the word *suffering* again. My purpose is not to focus on persecution and suffering—though it does come; in fact, it is unavoidable if we serve Christ. We have seen that when we demonstrate God's power the enemy will rise up against us. The difference is that when we serve God out of love and from our hearts rather than religious performance, the suffering is not our focus. Our focus remains on serving our King regardless of the consequences. Again, please take note that we are heirs of God and co-heirs with Christ. We actually share in His glory. But also notice verse 19, which states that creation waits in eager expectation for us to be revealed. It is time for us to manifest His Kingdom.

Did you notice that we are no longer in bondage? Yes! We have been brought into glorious freedom because we are children of God. It comes, however, through travail, as if we have been anointed to give birth to God's desire to bring forth His power in a new way. I believe that too often we expect Him simply to *break in* on us—when, in fact, He is waiting for us. He is aligning us with our purposes and destinies and waiting for us to cry out for His power to be demonstrated in our lives.

God's Mandate

God's mandate for mankind has never changed. We were born to take dominion and demonstrate His Kingdom on this earth. Remember that God's Word never returns to Him void. God's Word will always accomplish what it is sent to do. The Church is God's government operating in the earth, and guess what: The Church is not a building. You and I are the Church. We, as believers, are sons and daughters of God taking dominion and demonstrating His power on earth. Everything in me feels as if I am in travail, praying for the divine delivery of the supernatural. Just as a child is delivered through a narrow place, we are also coming forth through a narrow passage. Everything might seem tight and dark, but we must press on. We will come forth in power.

It is time for believers to come out of the closet. After all, everyone else is (and regarding everything imaginable—and they are unashamed!). I pray that we can be like Peter who never prayed to be delivered out of persecution, but prayed for more boldness.

My husband, Mickey, and I have made this our mandate for the season ahead. God has given me an anointing to pray for women with barren wombs. I have been using this gifting as we pray for barren situations to become fruitful. In the beginning of my ministry I witnessed miracles often, but then something happened—persecution—and I backed off. Now, I am approaching it again with great boldness. We may make mistakes, but we are not backing away any longer.

In the last few months, we have heard testimonies of backs being healed, legs growing out, bone spurs in the neck dissolving and chronic pain disappearing. One woman received her hearing (she had had ringing in her ears for years) as she walked into the doors of the church. Also, she had not been able to take deep breaths and, suddenly, she could breathe deeply and normally once more. I am believing for *more*. Mickey and I have witnessed tumors completely disappearing. One Vietnam veteran, whose ear was blown off in combat, was amazed to see it completely re-created. There are more testimonies occurring than I can write about. The point is, this is your mandate, too. It is true: Signs and wonders shall follow us who believe.

It is not about intelligence; it is not a twelve-step program for power: It is simple faith. It is also about believing that God is love. And because He loves us, He desires to break through our limitations and heal us.

In the Old Testament the word for *salvation* is *yeshuw'ah* (pronounced yesh-*oo*-aw), which means "saved, delivered, victorious, prosperous, healthy, helped"—all that we need. It is, in fact, the name of Jesus. It is evidence of Jesus' presence in both the Old and New Testaments. Before the foundation of the world, Jesus was slain, which provided salvation, deliverance, victory, prosperity, health, help and all that we could ever need. God's provision was planned since the beginning of time.

Though Adam and Eve sinned, God's original mandate for possessing the earth has not been changed. Sure, we have an enemy, but *sozo* promises us victory over every enemy of God. It is time to realize that we are people in the natural called to operate in the supernatural. It is time to access the supernatural and bring the government of heaven into the earth's realm.

Let me be blunt. Satan respects power, not preaching. Psalm 66 explains this clearly:

> Say to God, "How awesome are your deeds! So great is your power that your enemies cringe before you. All the earth bows down to you; they sing praise to you, they sing praise to your name."
>
> Psalm 66:3–4

Dear reader, our enemy cringes before the *power* of God. But until we decide to demonstrate that power, release from the grip of the enemy will not come. I encourage you to take time to read all of Psalm 66, as it will encourage you to be bold for Jesus. If we will cry out for power, He will give us deliverance.

And let's expect to take the spoils from our deliverance. God told Moses to display His power, and the strongman would let the people go—and not empty-handed either. The Egyptians gave the Israelites gold, silver and other riches when they were released from their bondage. This means that God has added up all that has been stolen from us, and we get it back—plus more.

When God gets vengeance, He gets personally involved in your release. Is that not wonderful? As you step out in divine authority, godly recompense goes into action.

Recompense for God's People

The word *recompense* means that "something has to be paid." Deuteronomy 32:35 talks about both vengeance and recompense as it states: "To me belongeth vengeance, and recompense" (KJV). Paul quotes this in his letter to the Romans: "Dearly beloved, avenge not yourselves, but rather give place unto wrath: for it is written, Vengeance is mine; I will repay, saith the Lord" (Romans 12:19 KJV).

Both the Old and New Testaments declare that God is a God of justice; He will punish our enemies. It is *His* responsibility and promise to us that He will do so. When He instructs us to lay hands on the sick and they shall recover, therefore, He is promising to judge sickness and release His divine healing as Jehovah-Rophe—God our Healer.

As I stated earlier, believers have something in common: We all know how to cry out! As we cry out, He promises to hear us. As a result, recompense comes. If you have ever been in bondage as a result of your limitations, you now have something coming to you as you step into a release of His demonstration and power. It was all settled at the cross. All you have to do is believe it and receive all that God has for you.

Crossing Over into the Promise

It is time to cross over into our promised lands and believe what God declares. (In chapter 11, I write further about the promised land of "rest.") When the Israelites crossed the Red Sea, Moses declared to them that they would never again have to fear the Egyptians (representing the past bondage). This is the word of the Lord for you now:

> Moses answered the people, "Do not be afraid. Stand firm and you will see the deliverance the LORD will bring you today. The Egyptians you see today you will never see again. The LORD will fight for you; you need only to be still."
>
> Exodus 14:13–14

Believer, regardless of what did not appear to work in the past, begin to believe that all things are possible *now.* Saying that you are full of God's power and that you are anointed to demonstrate that power will not make it happen. We must step up to the plate and truly believe. We each have a measure of faith—faith the size of a mustard seed is all we need. And simply believing that we are who God says we are is good use of that seed. Begin, right now, to know in your heart that you are God's child and have the life, love and light of God within you. You are one in Christ and He lives in you.

We are anointed children of the King, called to rule and reign with Christ. *So what is holding us back?* It is time to talk now about a strongman that manifests when we attempt to step out in power: the spirit of fear. This is what kept the Israelites from seeing themselves as God saw them. Remember? They saw themselves as grasshoppers.

Grasshoppers in Your Mirror

Imagine getting up one morning and looking in the mirror. But instead of seeing your own image, you see a big green grasshopper staring back at you. Ugh! Though very small in the natural, if inflated by the enemy this insect takes up the image of your entire being.

Well, we can laugh, but this ridiculous example shows how the enemy kept Israel from entering their Promised Land. When they saw or heard about the giants in their land (which God had already told them about, by the way), they saw themselves as grasshoppers. My question is, Who had the mirror that day? Whoever had it showed it to everyone but Joshua and Caleb—they never saw themselves as less than what God had said concerning them and their destiny (see Numbers 13).

This same type of spirit confronted David when he challenged Goliath. Goliath tried to intimidate him, but David knew who he was and never cowered. Thus, he was empowered to kill Goliath and cut his head off with his own giant sword.

What about Gideon? Remember, he is the one who said, "Who, me? Are you talking to me when you say 'mighty warrior'?" God prophesied to him and then whittled down his army. Numbers do not count when God wants glory. And, dear one, numbers never guarantee victory in God's war plans. So, if you have studied Gideon you realize that signs and wonders also followed him because he chose to "believe" in who God said He was.

It is time to defeat our defeated attitudes. Isaiah 61 declares that God's vengeance will defeat a spirit of heaviness when it tries to oppress us and keep us hidden (in the closet). Speak this passage over yourself. Every time I have italicized a word place your name there.

The Spirit of the Sovereign LORD is on *me*, because the LORD has anointed *me* to preach good news to the poor. He has sent *me* to bind up the brokenhearted, to proclaim freedom for the captives and release from darkness for the prisoners, to proclaim the year of the Lord's favor and the day of vengeance of our God, to comfort all who mourn, and provide for those who grieve in Zion—to bestow on them a crown of beauty instead of ashes, the oil of gladness instead of mourning, and a garment of praise instead of a spirit of despair. *They* will be called oaks of righteousness, a planting of the LORD for the display of his splendor.

They will rebuild the ancient ruins and restore the places long devastated; *they* will renew the ruined cities that have been devastated for generations. Aliens will shepherd *your* flocks; foreigners will work *your* fields and vineyards. And *you* will be called priests of the LORD, *you* will be named ministers of our God. *You* will feed on the wealth of nations, and in their riches *you* will boast.

Instead of *their* shame *my people* will receive a double portion, and instead of disgrace *they* will rejoice in *their* inheritance; and so *they* will inherit a double portion in *their* land, and everlasting joy will be *theirs*.

"For I, the LORD, love justice; I hate robbery and iniquity. In my faithfulness I will reward *them* and make an everlasting covenant with *them*. *Their* descendants will be known among the nations and *their* offspring among the peoples. All who see *them* will acknowledge that *they* are a people the LORD has blessed."

I delight greatly in the LORD; my soul rejoices in my God. For he has clothed *me* with garments of salvation and arrayed *me* in a robe of righteousness, as a bridegroom adorns his head like a priest, and as a bride adorns herself with her jewels. For as the soil makes the sprout come up and a garden causes seeds to grow, so the Sovereign LORD will make righteousness and praise spring up before all nations.

Isaiah 61:1–11 (emphasis added)

Dear one, I believe as you continue to declare this that you will come forth as a tree of righteousness and that all spirits of heaviness and fear will be defeated. Infirmity is also being defeated, because infirmity and heaviness are connected. I declare you healed, whole and completely restored in Jesus' name. *Sozo* is yours now!

Your Season of Favor

One morning while I was writing this book I awoke and heard the Lord speak this passage to my heart (note that it is in both the Old and New Testaments):

> For He says, In the time of favor (of an assured welcome) I have listened to and heeded your call, and I have helped you on the day of deliverance (the day of salvation). Behold, now is truly the time for a gracious welcome and acceptance [of you from God]; behold, now is the day of salvation! [Isa. 49:8.]
>
> 2 Corinthians 6:2 AMPLIFIED

Precious believer, this is our season of favor and salvation (*sozo*). While we are in our season of favor, the Lord desires to provide answers. He is listening and is heeding us as we cry out to Him. He is giving us total acceptance—no matter what we have done in the past, we are forgiven. Hallelujah!

But, there is more—so much more. Psalm 30:5 states that His favor lasts a lifetime. Though we weep for a night, joy will always come in the morning. God is stating to us that He is turning mourning into dancing. All grief and sorrow must flee as we fully understand the grace of God that is upon us right now to experience the supernatural.

I recall the time that my mother was diagnosed with lung cancer 25 years ago. One night we rushed her to the emergency room because she was vomiting blood. She spent several days in the hospital, and the doctors were planning on removing one-third of both lungs plus place her on chemotherapy. Mom asked for two days at home before the surgery and requested one more biopsy (believing God for a miracle in between). So she went home and we, as a family, gathered around her and prayed a simple prayer of faith. There was no *known* presence of angels, though I do believe they were present, and none of us felt especially anointed at the time. But my sister, Pam, rose up with great faith and cursed the cancer to the root. Then, when the prayer was over we went home and prepared ourselves for Mom's biopsy the next day.

The next morning I must have had to stop at *every* traffic light along the way—bottom line, I was late for her biopsy. When I arrived at the surgery waiting room, Mom's doctor was looking at a glass jar with something inside. I asked the doctor if he had done the biopsy, and he said he had. I explained how sorry I was for being late, but he acted as if I were not even there. His entire focus was on this "thing" in this glass jar.

Cutting to the chase here, during the biopsy Mom coughed and the cancerous tumor completely dislodged, and it was described by the doctor as having been "coughed up." The cancerous tumor ended up in his biopsy jar. And the doctor said that the location of the root of the cancer was immediately covered over with fresh, new pink skin. He actually saw fresh pink skin cover the hole where the root had been. He exclaimed, "This is a miracle!" Well, you can imagine our rejoicing. When Mom found out she jumped off the table and went up and down the halls screaming, "Jesus healed me! Jesus healed me!"

I still have a picture that the doctor gave me of the cancer and its root in that glass jar. I think it is time to believe for miracles again and for them to follow us who continue to believe.

Unlimited Potential

God has created each of us with unlimited potential to do the supernatural. Your potential is limitless, open-ended, cannot be measured. There is no IQ test that can evaluate either your potential or your intelligence when God gets involved. It is all about knowing who you are in Christ. The Lord desires to move you beyond the limitations of a grasshopper mentality.

I hear people ask, "What if I pray for people and they are not healed?" My response is, "What if they are?" Sure, we will make some mistakes along the way of learning, but it is worth the risk. When someone is healed, you realize how little you had to do with it other than obedience. The rest is up to Him. You do your part—He promises to do His.

God says that our thoughts are not His thoughts and His ways are not our ways. He loves surprises—have you noticed? It is time to disregard and reject every single thought, counsel, idea or imagination that has conflicted with what God says about you. The devil loves to discredit you and your potential. He loves to shrink-wrap your vision into a tiny fruit basket. But let me assure you of this one thing: As you are reading this book there is a supernatural pregnancy in the air. You are being overshadowed by God to be a demonstrator of His glory. Become someone who begins to meditate on His promises and get a mental picture of your potential and victory.

The Israelites got a mental picture of themselves as grasshoppers. What is your mental picture? Is it different? Well, then, that is how you will respond. Choose the valid one—the one that God says you are.

Time for Reflection

1. When you picture yourself, what do you see? Weakness, fear, intimidation? Do you realize these lies are from the enemy? God sees you as powerful, His child and His heir created in His own image. Write below the lie of the enemy and then what God says about you.

   This is the lie that I have believed:

   _____

   _____

   _____

   This is what God says concerning me:

   _____

   _____

   _____

2. What causes you to fear praying for others? Can you identify it? If so, write it below:

   _____

   _____

   _____

Now pick out a passage from Scripture where the apostles prayed for others who were healed or delivered or even raised from the dead. Write the passages below and mentally picture yourself praying for others and God touching them in a powerful way.

_____

_____

_____

3. Consider Gideon right now. God called him a mighty warrior; Gideon basically responded, "Who, me?" Have you done that? Now that you have read this book so far, can you respond differently? Write your testimony below and share it with others.

_____

_____

_____

Remember, a testimony is basically saying, "Do it again, Lord." Never negate the power of your testimony. Share it over and over and over. You are causing the atmosphere to become pregnant with God's ability to do it again. Right now, before turning the page, write down at least three people you will call and share your testimony with:

1. _____

2. _____

3. _____

7

The Benefits of Being a Living Sacrifice

Letting Go of Squelched Passion

There is hardly a clearer example than the apostle Paul of someone who experienced a renewed mind. Once he met Jesus on that road to Damascus and broke free from the bonds of legalism and Pharisaism, he experienced amazing transformation.

Just so, our minds have to be renewed in order to understand the power of God's grace and His righteousness. In fact, we experience transformation (the renewing of our minds) every time we hear the Word and receive revelation from God. This renewing of our minds is strongly connected to repentance because when we repent we "change our minds." When we "repent and turn away from sin" we become more and more transformed.

We have already discussed the fact that we are righteous *only* due to the finished work of Christ at the cross, and that legalism limits us from moving in power by offering a false sense of security—the expectation that our works can justify or vindicate us. Paul now takes us a step further in our understanding.

Paul tells us that only when our minds are renewed are we able to test and approve what God's perfect will is for our lives. Our transformation hinges on this renewing. But how does this renewing take place? Look at his words:

> Therefore, I urge you, brothers, in view of God's mercy, to *offer your bodies as living sacrifices*, holy and pleasing to God—this is your spiritual act of worship. Do not conform any longer to the pattern of this world, but *be transformed by the renewing of your mind*. Then you will be able to test and approve what God's will is—his good, pleasing and perfect will.
>
> Romans 12:1–2 (emphasis added)

We are transformed as our minds are renewed, and this renewing of the mind takes place as we "offer our bodies as living sacrifices." Paul experienced this need (burden) throughout his life and ministry.

In this chapter, we will discuss what it means to be a living sacrifice. This is a concept that sometimes stirs fear in our hearts, but that is not what God intends. He longs for us to know His passion in serving. Let's see how this concept of being a living sacrifice helps us break through our fears and experience His power at work in us.

The Body

Even as a child I took seriously Paul's admonition that we must present our bodies as living sacrifices, for this is holy and pleasing to God. I can remember being in Sunday school and thinking that to please God I had to become a missionary and travel to some foreign land. That was a frightening thought—but it certainly seemed the "religious thing" I might be required to do to be a worthy living sacrifice. I thank the Lord that He breathed upon me the revelation that my "assignment" from Him was personally designed for me—and it is the same for you. Each of us has his or her own "assignment page" in God's "assignment book."

Yet the term *sacrifice* surely suggests that there might be hardship in our service. Nothing is completely convenient when we serve God. Before you think you should stop reading this chapter, allow me to explain. Sacrifice is the natural outcome of a passionate heart to serve. Not only do we not gain anything from a religious "works" mentality, which tries to "die more to self" in hopes of pleasing God, but true servanthood—sacrifice—actually pays huge dividends. I have learned that my passion to serve God comes from my being the "wood on the altar of sacrifice."

Let's start with this concept of passion in this process of transformation.

Our Passion and God's Power

To fully experience and demonstrate God's supernatural power, we must have a sustaining passion. Why? Because when persecution arises, we have a tendency to shrink back. One of the most powerful works of the enemy is to limit our passion and, by doing so, stifle our effectiveness for serving God. It has been my experience that the devil uses one particularly powerful spirit to limit our passion from taking expression. This archenemy is the Jezebel spirit.

I have written extensively concerning Jezebel, and will not go into too much detail here, but let me assure you that just as this spirit attacked Elijah in his passion to tear down false altars and speak prophetic words, so this spirit will attack us. Jeremiah had an anointing similar to Elijah's. Scripture describes Jeremiah's calling not only as one who would speak for God as prophet, but also as one who would "uproot, tear down, destroy, overthrow" and "build up."

> The word of the LORD came to me, saying, "Before I formed you in the womb I knew you, before you were born I set you apart; I appointed you as a prophet to the nations. . . . See, today I appoint you over nations and kingdoms to uproot and tear down, to destroy and overthrow, to build and to plant."
>
> Jeremiah 1:4–5, 10

As far as having the ability to see prophetically, I am aware that I have that same calling upon my life. And you, dear one, even if you do not have a specific prophetic gifting, are part of God's "prophetic people." *Prophetic people* are those who *hear* God's voice, *know* God's voice and *follow* His voice. Yes, that means you! Point to yourself and say, "I am anointed of God to uproot powers of darkness, to tear down false idols and counterfeit belief systems, to destroy powers of darkness, to build God's Kingdom and plant seeds of His love and seeds of truth into the hearts of God's people."

This also means, however, that you are a target of the Jezebel spirit. Our challenge begins with *seeing* ourselves moving in demonstration and power, and believing that

God is transforming us as we move forward in Him. Go for it. You and I will never be more equipped, anointed and appointed than we are right now this very minute to be used by God. This is not to imply that you do not need to study God's Word or be trained in some particular ministry. What it does mean is that as a believer you are already anointed because Jesus Christ, the Anointed One, lives *in* you.

It was a wonderful day for me when I realized that I did not have to go to Asia or Africa to use my gifting. If travel to foreign lands is your calling, then you will have passion to achieve it—or you might simply be called to encourage someone on the phone today. The point is that allowing Him to use you puts you in the category of *living sacrifice* and that your passion will be in alignment with it.

Okay. Let's look at passion. Recently I have been crying out for a greater fiery presence of God without understanding why. Actually, I do not want any more fire; I have been on the potter's wheel and thrown into that kiln more times than I can count. But when my passion wavers, I notice I cry out for more of His fiery presence. *Passion changes our view of sacrifice. Being a living sacrifice for Him is much easier and more pleasurable whenever it is coupled with passion.*

The book of Revelation talks about Jesus' eyes being as fire as He is addressing the church of Thyatira. In fact, He introduces Himself to the church of Thyatira like this: "To the angel of the church in Thyatira write: These are the words of the Son of God, whose *eyes are like blazing fire* and whose feet are like burnished bronze" (Revelation 2:18, emphasis added).

Do you find Jesus' description of Himself interesting? Why did He present Himself this way to this particular church? It is my belief that He was addressing the passion (fiery presence) needed to overcome the Jezebel spirit, which that church tolerated.

Dear one, to have passion for the work we are called to do, we must let Jesus renew our minds—by becoming living sacrifices—so that He can do His transforming work within us. If we let fear rule in our hearts—fear of laying our lives on His altar—we can be sure that the enemy will take advantage of every opportunity. But if we let passion guide us, then like Paul, Elijah and Jeremiah, we will overcome fear and experience God's power.

Returning to Our First Love

Elijah teaches us something further about this passion: how to maintain it. If you remember from the biblical account of his confrontation with the prophets of Baal on Mt. Carmel, supernatural fire came from heaven to consume the sacrifice that Elijah had placed on the altar. We are no longer under the Law with its obligation to sacrifice animals, but the concept of an altar has not disappeared. God has stated that He writes His law on our hearts. This means that, for believers today, our hearts are His altar. What is the sacrifice? Our very lives.

In Revelation 2:1–8 Jesus addressed the church of Ephesus and pointed out that they had left their first love. In other words, there was no more passion to serve God. Think on this: When two people are in love, passion is definitely burning. It is hard to keep two lovers separated from each other, right? They cannot wait to spend time with each other.

For us to offer our bodies as living sacrifices requires that same burning passion. It means that we cannot wait to spend time with God. We want to do what He is doing. We want to be involved with the missions He is leading. This is the kind of passion that results in power to further His Kingdom and demonstrate His love to others.

And it starts by understanding that sacrifice attracts fire. When Elijah made the sacrifice, he placed the offering on the altar and fire fell from heaven to consume it. God's fire will *always* fall upon a sacrifice of a pure heart. Jesus' eyes of fire are ready right now to consume your sacrifice as you worship Him in Spirit and truth. In other words, simply offering our lives as sacrifices will ignite passion for our callings.

There are times that I walk in this kind of passion, where I long for nothing more than His purifying presence. But I have to confess that my passion for being a sacrifice comes and goes. Perhaps you experience that as well. I know now that this passion needs to be sustained, but how does that happen? How is it sustained through the ups and downs of life?

Well, let's look again at the sacrificial offerings in the Old Testament. Not only did every offering placed on the altar undergo fire, but Leviticus 6:9 states that the fire was supposed to burn on the altar *continuously* until the offering was completely consumed. We might say that the fire burned with passion as long as the sacrifice was on the altar. Just so, Jesus' fire consumes and purifies *continuously* the sacrificial offerings made from our hearts.

Jesus came to set us free, to offer us *sozo* to the fullest. He dances over us with singing and rejoices over us with divine passion. The term *Passion Week* (observed during the Lenten season) describes Jesus' wrenching sacrifice during the week He approached the cross and completely fulfilled the Law. It was His passion to die for us—to become the Lamb slain for our sins so that we might be reconciled to the Father—that helped Him set His face like flint toward the cross. Christ finished well, indeed!

The Lord has recently laid it upon my heart that I am not simply to run the race but I am also to "finish well." Dear one, it is also important that you finish well. How do we do that? Remember this important fact: God will never *not* pursue you. He is continually perfecting us into His divine image.

Even with ups and downs, we will finish well if we remain committed to allowing God to demonstrate His power and the supernatural through us. It will take burning, unquenched passion to continue this race we are running. Remember, then, that sacrifice attracts fire and that fire ignites passion. As you lay your life on the altar, you will be strengthened to endure and accomplish all that is assigned for you to do for His glory. And, dear one, always keep in mind that obedience is always a sacrifice. We need to rely on God's grace to empower us to remain obedient, for we cannot be obedient in our own strength. Becoming a living sacrifice is what it takes to finish well.

Let's look now more closely at how this helps our minds be renewed.

Opening the Gates

God wants to ignite fiery passion within our hearts so that we experience—and demonstrate—His transforming power. In our discussion of the body as an instrument of sacrifice, it follows that when our hearts are touched by His

Spirit, and we allow His law to be written on our hearts, He begins to renew our minds. In fact, our minds cannot be renewed and we cannot be transformed until God has changed our hearts. When we give genuine praise to God, praise that is based upon Spirit and Truth, our hearts are aligned with His heart and then our minds are made new.

Since our bodies are God's temples and our hearts His altars, we can look at Scripture to understand the symbolism of gates through which the Lord enters. Isaiah 60, in particular, talks about the future glory of Zion and the Lord's entrance there. "No longer will violence be heard in your land, nor ruin or destruction within your borders, but you will call your *walls* Salvation and your *gates* Praise" (Isaiah 60:18, emphasis added). In much the same way, He desires to enter the gates and walls of our hearts as we give Him praise and trust in His salvation (*sozo*).

The most important gates in the city of Jerusalem were those that led in and out of the Temple of God. Granted, entrance through the gates of Jerusalem itself was significant, but spiritually the gates or doorways to His Temple were of utmost importance.

The Temple faced east. The entryway was hung with double wooden doors layered with Corinthian bronze. Imagine the brilliance each morning when the sun arose and struck those eastern gates. It must have reminded the people of the brilliance of the glory of God. When God finds an entrance into the gates of our hearts, we will shine forth His glory as well. What can destroy our effectiveness? Religion, false doctrine, wrong mindsets, hardness of heart.

If you recall, Jesus spoke directly to the disciples asking if their hearts were still hardened after all He had taught them. Hard hearts make place for "the leaven of the Pharisees, and . . . the leaven of Herod" (see Mark 8:15; more on leaven in chapter 8). When you co-labor with God, your heart beats with His heart regarding the assignments He has laid out for you.

Taking this one step further, we look at the twelve gates of the New Jerusalem. Scripture describes them this way: "And the twelve gates were twelve pearls, each separate gate being built of one solid pearl. And the main street (the broadway) of the city was of gold as pure and translucent as glass" (Revelation 21:21 AMPLIFIED).

Do you know how a pearl is formed within an oyster? A grain of sand gets into the shell and irritates the flesh of the oyster. It secretes layer after layer of smooth coating to ease the friction and irritation. Sound familiar? Irritation, friction . . . persecution? You can rejoice in this fact that whenever Satan is instigating any type of friction, God will use it to build a *gate* of praise with walls of *salvation* and keep the fire burning on the altar. Every time the enemy initiates persecution, bring forth the sacrifice of praise and be strengthened in the Lord as He consumes that sacrifice. Unfortunately, when we are in the midst of turmoil or friction, we do not feel like praising God. This is when it becomes a sacrifice. All the while, though, God keeps the fires of passion burning.

Allow God access through the gate of your heart right now. Just make this confession:

Lord, I want to shine for You on this earth. I desire for my heart to become a gate of entrance for Your glory. It is my desire to demonstrate Your power on earth. I pray as Jesus taught the disciples to pray—that Your will be done on earth as it is in heaven. Use me, Lord. Please show me any area in my heart that might have become hardened. Cleanse the leaven from my thoughts, my life and my heart. I ask this in the name of Jesus, my Lord and Savior, Amen.

More on Transformation

Allow me to take a moment and define transformation or what it means to be transformed. Romans 12:2 says:

> Do not be conformed to this world (this age), [fashioned after and adapted to its external, superficial customs], but be transformed (changed) by the [entire] renewal of your mind [by its new ideals and its new attitude], so that you may prove [for yourselves] what is the good and acceptable and perfect will of God, even the thing which is good and acceptable and perfect [in His sight for you].
>
> AMPLIFIED

I enjoy reading this in the Amplified Version because it becomes clearer that transformation involves change, and that change (in us) comes by renewing the mind. When our minds are renewed we are open to receiving new ideas taught to us by the Holy Spirit. It means that we let go of the limitations that hold us from receiving His truths. The word *transformed* is the Greek word *metamorphoo* (where we get our English word *metamorphosis*) and means "to change and be formed." *Transformation* means "metamorphosis"—such as when a caterpillar is transformed into a beautiful butterfly.

For too long, many Christians have been taught wrong theology concerning the mind—as if our minds are not really important or are even a hindrance. Many preachers, for instance, tell us not to listen to what our minds say, or to be led by our "hearts" and not our "heads." The problem with this, however, is that our minds must be important because God speaks about them quite often. What He desires, of course, is a mind that is *renewed*. When Jesus brought His world into ours, He came with a message of repentance— which we know means to *change your mind*. Transformation involves just that—a change of mind, a new understanding or renewal of what is true brought to our thinking processes.

We are being awakened to a *new norm*, as I term it. What used to be the *normal* Christian has been invaded by God's power and revelation. His Kingdom involves an entirely different government, one that releases divine authority to us as believers—thus giving us power over spirits of darkness, sickness and disease, poverty, etc. Though many of us in times past have experienced the supernatural—casting out devils and allowing God to use us in demonstrating the miraculous—God wants to *invade* our lives completely and demonstrate His power and love radically.

Correct doctrine should include the demonstration of His power rather than legalistic mindsets. By saying that, I mean that if our doctrine does not involve the supernatural, then our doctrine is void of power. One can read the New Testament and never camp out with Jesus and experience His demonstration of power. In fact, many preachers simply skip over the chapters that mention the supernatural power Jesus demonstrated and declare that miracles died with the apostles.

We, as believers, must redefine what is *normal* for Christians. When Jesus said to pray that God's will be done on earth as it is in heaven, He was saying to pray for what is in heaven to be normal on earth. There is no sickness in heaven—it should not be *here*. There is no lack in heaven—it should not be *here*. The will of God is not difficult to understand. It is simple: "Thy will be done in earth, as it is in heaven" (Matthew 6:10).

Changed Hearts and Minds

When the Bible speaks about renewing the mind, it suggests nothing short of battle. This is because our minds get in the way and we attempt to rationalize God's supernatural intervention. It is easy—even tempting—to rationalize Scripture and try to understand God intellectually. The supernatural, however, is never understood through the intellect; the process of understanding the supernatural is first birthed in the heart, and then the mind begins to be renewed to the truth of the Gospel. Transformation cannot occur unless our hearts are changed and our minds renewed.

We gain some insight concerning transformation when we read of Christ being transfigured as He talked with Moses and Elijah (see Mark 9:2–8). Picture it: the glory of heaven and its reality visible through Jesus. A completely different world, usually not seen by our natural eyes, was revealed through this transformation. Dear one, transformation is also here for us—though unseen now, it will manifest as we demonstrate His power. The word *transformed* in that passage is the same word used in Romans 12:2 about the mind being renewed. The renewed mind is one of the ways that God transforms us; it is a reality of another world—God's world. When He lives in us, the Light of the world (Jesus) shines brightly in us and, because of Him, we reveal the glory of God.

As I mentioned earlier, many Christians have downplayed the importance of the mind. We have been taught to not trust what we think—to distrust our minds. We have been told that God cannot be understood in our heads, but only in our hearts. Granted, we cannot let our minds dictate to our spirits, but neither can we simply toss out the capacity that God has given us in our minds—once they are renewed.

The Pharisees thought that their great learning was the key to spiritual superiority, but their minds were not renewed. Thus, when Jesus came crashing into their theology and confronted those brilliant biblical scholars, they could not recognize Him for who He was. If we are going to be transformed and experience His Kingdom, we need both mind and heart. We need a renewed mind—a sanctified mind, the mind of Christ—and hearts that long to serve Him.

It takes work to renew the mind. It requires fellowship and intimacy with God. Few pay the price—few become that living sacrifice. Those who choose to reject the renewed mind will be of little use to the Lord—little demonstration and power will flow from an unrenewed mind, for it follows that that life will not be transformed.

So Where Do We Start?

To be transformed—to have an open heart and renewed mind, and to be positioned with power and authority—starts with repentance. *Return to God and return to His way of thinking.* Return to His reality. Have more faith in what is unseen than in what is seen. Jesus is offering His Kingdom to us, but if we never change the way we think, we will not experience it. We will still go to heaven—but we will not walk in Kingdom power in the here and now on earth.

The only way to experience heaven on earth is to change the way we think concerning the supernatural. Once our hearts fully embrace the truth that God desires to invade our world with His supernatural power to heal, restore, protect and save, we will witness His Kingdom manifesting on earth. It is about putting off the old man and putting on the new. Kingdom living cannot be separated from that concept. Dear one, heaven is now!

Time for Reflection

1. Renewing the mind is about believing what God said even though we are not witnessing the results yet. Be assured that though we may not see it, God is still working behind the scenes. Our trust must remain in His Word—no matter what. Write a promise that God has given you that seems unfulfilled. Then, after writing that seemingly unfulfilled promise, write below it what the Word of God states concerning that situation.

Lord, I am not seeing this promise fulfilled:

But Your Word says this about Kingdom living, and I choose to believe Your Word:

_____

_____

_____

2. Describe, below, what happens in your mind when you need a miracle or some type of breakthrough. Then, write a personal prayer to the Lord asking Him to renew your mind. Be watchful for any needed repentance as you write.

Lord, this is what my mind tells me when I need a miracle or a breakthrough:

_____

_____

_____

But Your Word says that I can renew my mind concerning your faithfulness. I repent (change my mind) and believe in Your Word. (Write this in your own words.)

_____

_____

_____

3. Describe ways in which you can become a *living sacrifice* for God. Do you need passion? Ask the Lord for His fiery presence that will sustain you day after day, week after week, month after month and year after year!

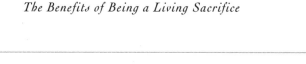

Now, before moving on, I need to talk to you straight. Simply reading through this book, going through repentance and writing down a few declarations does not mean that you are instantly 100 percent transformed and that you never have to study His Word again. No way, precious one. God is transforming us daily, maybe hourly. Remember, He is not limited to time. It is safe to say, therefore, that He is forever changing us into His image.

Some of you reading this book may feel condemned because you realize you have believed falsehoods concerning God and His goodness. Condemnation is not my intent. My hope and my purpose for writing are to help you enter into His divine presence so that you can be transformed into His image. We are told in the Word that we move from glory to glory. This book is all about moving forward into more of His glory. With that in mind, get ready to learn about Kingdom miracles.

8

There Is a Miracle in You!

Letting Go of a Hardened Heart

Brace yourself. I really mean it. You need to prepare your heart for this chapter because this particular one will challenge any area of spiritual apathy. And additionally, you will be required to do some inner housecleaning because as you continue to read you will most likely be led to repent as the Holy Spirit ministers to you. As you glean from God's Word and gain new revelation, the renewing of your mind continues to occur. A renewed mind will always give credibility to the power of God being demonstrated through you.

Want to run now? Desiring to skip this chapter and move to another? Hold tight. This is where you get a divine opportunity to know in your mind and truly understand in your heart that you are destined to minister in *power*.

Yes, just as this chapter title says—there is a miracle in you. Not just *for* you, but also *in* you!

The disciples learned this. Maybe you have been like me and read the story of the feeding of the four thousand—Jesus' *second* miraculous feeding of a great crowd—and never realized that the disciples were very much involved in this miracle (see Matthew 15:32–39). In fact, if they had not believed that Jesus' miracle-working power would operate in them as He blessed the food, they would never have taken the small portions He handed them and moved forward with faith to feed the multitudes.

Yes, a miracle occurred—partly because of their obedience, partly because of their faith. Scripture states that Jesus prayed, blessed and broke the food. It was the disciples who performed the miracle as the food was passed out to the thousands. Never heard that preached before? Look closely at the New Living Translation:

> About this time another great crowd had gathered, and the people ran out of food again. Jesus called his disciples and told them, "I feel sorry for these people. They have been here with me for three days, and they have nothing left to eat. And if I send them home without feeding them, they will faint along the road. For some of them have come a long distance."
>
> "How are we supposed to find enough food for them here in the wilderness?" his disciples asked.
>
> "How many loaves of bread do you have?" he asked.
>
> "Seven," they replied. So Jesus told all the people to sit down on the ground. Then he took the seven loaves, thanked God for them, broke them into pieces, and gave them to his disciples, who distributed the bread to the

crowd. A few small fish were found, too, so Jesus also blessed these and told the disciples to pass them out.

They ate until they were full, and when the scraps were picked up, there were seven large baskets of food left over! There were about four thousand people in the crowd that day, and he sent them home after they had eaten.

Mark 8:1–9 NLT

Now let's back up and see how the disciples became positioned to perform such a miracle, and, yet, how their hardened hearts caused them—even after they had experienced the power of Jesus working through them—to miss the message that *there was a miracle in them to perform.* Keep reading. I will point out that they just did not "get it." No, they didn't comprehend that they were individually involved in the miracle.

The First Miraculous Feeding

Jesus, whose ministry was becoming well-known in the surrounding cities and villages, had just been told of the death of John the Baptist at the hands of King Herod. As soon as He heard the news, Jesus told His disciples to come with Him to a quiet place away from the crowds for a while so they could rest. "For there were many coming and going, and they did not even have time to eat" (Mark 6:31 NKJV).

They climbed into their boat and tried to slip quietly away across the Sea of Galilee—but the crowds were not so easily discouraged. People from the surrounding towns saw where the little band was headed and, by running ahead along the shore, they actually arrived first. Thus, when the boat landed, Jesus saw the great multitude and, rather than taking time to rest, was "moved with compassion for them, because they were like sheep not having a shepherd. So He began to teach them many things" (Mark 6:34 NKJV).

Finally the day was spent, but Jesus had one more lesson to teach. In their haste to follow Jesus, apparently, the thousands of people had not brought food with them. The disciples encouraged Jesus to send them on their way, out of that deserted place, to go buy bread in the surrounding villages. The story of the feeding of the five thousand men—"in addition to all the women and children!" (Matthew 14:21 NLT)—is given in all four Gospels: Matthew 14:13–21; Mark 6:30-44; Luke 9:10–17; and John 6:1–15. Let's follow Mark's account here.

> He answered and said to them, "You give them something to eat." And they said to Him, "Shall we go and buy two hundred denarii worth of bread and give them something to eat?"
>
> But He said to them, "How many loaves to you have? Go and see." And when they found out they said, "Five, and two fish."
>
> Then He commanded them to make them all sit down in groups on the green grass. So they sat down in ranks, in hundreds and in fifties. And when He had taken the five loaves and the two fish, He looked up to heaven, blessed and broke the loaves, and gave them to His disciples to set before them; and the two fish He divided among them all. So they all ate and were filled. And they took up twelve baskets full of fragments and of the fish. Now those who had eaten the loaves were about five thousand men.
>
> Mark 6:37–44 NKJV

In the New Living Translation, two of the accounts of this miracle say this: "Breaking the loaves into pieces, [Jesus] *kept giving* the bread and fish to the disciples to give to the people" (Mark 6:41 NLT, emphasis added). And: "Breaking the loaves into pieces, [Jesus] *kept giving* the bread and fish to the disciples to give to the people" (Luke 9:16 NLT, emphasis added).

We will see why this wording is significant when we return to the story of the second miraculous feeding—that of the four thousand.

The Storm at Sea

Now let's focus on what limited the disciples' understanding that there was a miracle in them. If we read on, we see that Jesus, while sending the crowds away, instructed His disciples to get into the boat and sail across the lake toward Bethsaida (see Mark 6:45), which, by the way, means "house of fish." (I love how the Lord tucks in little reminders along our journey with Him to reinforce His life-lessons.)

Jesus then went up into the hills to pray alone, and the disciples obediently sailed off in their boat toward their next destination.

When it was evening, the boat was in the middle of the sea, and He was alone on the land. Seeing them straining at the oars, for the wind was against them, at about the fourth watch of the night He came to them, walking on the sea; and He intended to pass by them. But when they saw Him walking on the sea, they supposed that it was a ghost, and cried out; for they all saw Him and were terrified. But immediately He spoke with them and said to them, "Take courage; it is I, do not be afraid." *Then He got into the boat with them, and the wind stopped; and they were utterly astonished, for they had not gained any insight from the incident of the loaves, but their heart was hardened.*

Mark 6:47–52 NASB (emphasis added)

A terrible storm arose. Matthew 14:24 says that "the disciples were in trouble far away from land, for a strong wind had risen, and they were fighting heavy waves" (NLT). Jesus saw that they were rowing hard, and at about three in the morning He came to them, walking on the water. When the disciples saw Him through the wind and waves, they screamed in terror thinking he was a ghost.

Now, let's take a moment and think about this. They had spent a great deal of time with Jesus; yet when fear struck their hearts, they could not recognize Him. Is that not how we often are? When fearful, we forget what Jesus looks like. By this I think it is very safe to say that He looks just like His Word. He *is* the Word—that is what He looks like. Since the Word states that He is my healer, I see Him healing my body. Since the Word states that He is my provider, I see Him meeting my every need. Since the Word says that He is my peace, I see every storm in my life calmed as I focus on the Prince of Peace.

Picture yourself in the boat with the disciples. You have witnessed with them the miraculous feeding of five thousand men plus thousands of women and children, and now you are rubbing elbows with them. A storm gathers and, like them, you are afraid for your life. What happened to the memory of the miracle Jesus performed that very afternoon? Could it be that you, like the disciples, have a hard heart because you do not fully understand that Jesus *really is* who He says He is? If He can provide food miraculously, can He not also save me in the midst of a storm?

The disciples could not comprehend it. Their hearts were hard. The Word states that they had not "gained any insight" or "considered" (KJV) the feeding of the multitudes. Dear one, what we "consider" is what we give our attention to. Not "considering" or "gaining insight" to what God has done in our lives will produce hard hearts.

And, please think on this. Jesus was about to "pass them by." Ouch! Why was that? It would be like us reminding the Lord that we have a house payment due Friday, and He passes us by while we are terrified during a storm on Wednesday. Could it be that Jesus expects us to *consider* the miraculous provision He has provided in the past?

Jesus calmed their fears and got into the boat with them. As He did, the storm also calmed. Precious one, there is always peace when Jesus is with us. I do not ever want to leave shore without Him. Do you?

The "Bread of Life"

Jesus, having just broken the bread for the vast multitude of five thousand-plus the day before, would now use bread as a symbol for teaching the returning crowds. It was nearing time for the annual Passover celebration (see John 6:4), and Jewish families would be removing leaven from their homes in preparation. Leaven represents sin, and Jesus used this image to teach His disciples further about the legalism.

It was morning. After their harrowing night at sea, the disciples landed at Gennesaret (see Mark 6:53). Back across the lake, the crowds were starting to return to the place where they had last seen Jesus, for they knew His disciples had departed without Him, and they expected Him to come down the mountainside any moment. (This story is told in John 6:22–59.)

But He did not appear. Finally they sailed across the lake to look for Him and, we might assume, were very surprised to see Him there with His disciples.

Here Scripture gives Jesus' wonderful teaching about Himself as the Bread of Life. He discerned that they were basically following Him in order to get another meal, and used the opportunity to tell them that they could have "the true bread from heaven" (John 6:32).

The people, however, murmured against Jesus for calling Himself bread from heaven, for they agreed that they certainly knew where He came from—and it was not heaven. But then Jesus gave them an even harder message to comprehend: Not only was He bread from heaven, but they had to "eat" this bread in order to have eternal life.

Even Jesus' followers had trouble with this teaching. Later, Jesus knew that they were complaining among themselves, so He said to them, "Does this offend you? Then what will you think if you see me, the Son of Man, return to heaven again? It is the spirit who gives eternal life. Human effort accomplishes nothing" (John 6:61–63 NLT). It was at this point that "many of His disciples turned away and deserted Him" (John 6:66 NLT).

Jesus travelled on with His disciples to Tyre and to Sidon and then back to the Sea of Galilee where, once again, a large hungry crowd would gather. This brings us to the feeding of the four thousand, and the lesson that it is the presence of Jesus that leads to miracle-working power. Amazingly, because of their hard hearts, the disciples still fail to understand.

Small Portions Multiplied

At the opening of this chapter we read the story of feeding the four thousand. Notice again the part of the disciples:

> Jesus told all the people to sit down on the ground. Then he took the seven loaves, thanked God for them, broke them into pieces, and gave them to his disciples, who distributed the bread to the crowd. A few small fish were found, too, so Jesus also blessed these and told the disciples to pass them out.
>
> Mark 8:6–7 NLT

In the feeding of the five thousand, we read that Jesus "kept giving" out pieces of bread and fish. In this story, I believe He broke the available bread and fish into small pieces and sent the disciples off with instructions to feed the crowds *themselves* from those small portions.

My husband, who has also taught from this text and whom I need to credit for the title of the chapter, did a mathematical calculation concerning exactly how much the disciples had in each basket with which to feed so many people. Each of the twelve began with a very small portion, less than .17 of a piece of a fish (less than a quarter) and close to .42 of a loaf (less than half). Yet each one witnessed an increase each time he reached into his basket. In fact, Scripture says the people ate until they could hold no more—I think the word *stuffed* might fit this situation.

There were even seven large baskets left on the grass (Jesus had provided also for their future!). Dear one, there was a miracle in them and they did not even know it—not during the meal or after the meal.

How sad that even after the disciples had witnessed the miraculous, they still did not *get it*. What I mean is that they did not comprehend what had really happened *through* them with the feeding of the four thousand and how much miracle-working power God had given them.

Jesus used an encounter with the Pharisees to try to help them understand:

> Now those who had eaten were about four thousand. And He sent them away, immediately got into the boat with His disciples, and came to the region of Dalmanutha. Then the Pharisees came out and began to dispute with Him, seeking from Him a sign from heaven, testing Him. But He sighed deeply in His spirit, and said, "Why does this generation seek a sign? . . ." And He left them, and getting into the boat again, departed to the other side.
>
> Mark 8:9–13 NKJV

The Pharisees once again question Jesus. Interesting, is it not, that after a miracle the religious spirits question a move of the Holy Spirit? Jesus got into the boat with the disciples again, and they discovered that they had only one loaf of bread with them. They had left the seven baskets behind! But, more significantly, they forgot that Jesus, the Bread of Life, was with them all along. Their focus was on the natural, and as He was attempting to shift their minds to think supernaturally, He pointed out their hard hearts. Notice here the leaven that Jesus warned about:

Now the disciples had forgotten to take bread, and they did not have more than one loaf with them in the boat. Then He charged them, saying, "Take heed, beware of the leaven of the Pharisees and the leaven of Herod." And they *reasoned* among themselves, saying, "It is because we have not bread." But Jesus, being aware of it, said to them, . . . "Do you not yet perceive nor understand? Is your heart still hardened? Having eyes, do you not see? And having ears, do you not hear? And do you not remember? When I broke the five loaves for the five thousand, how many baskets full of fragments did you take up?"

They said to Him, "Twelve."

"Also, when I broke the seven for the four thousand, how many large baskets full of fragments did you take up?"

And they said, "Seven."

So He said to them, "How is it you do not understand?"

Mark 8:14–21 NKJV, emphasis added

As you read this passage, did you notice that when Jesus mentioned leaven, the disciples *reasoned* that Jesus must be referring to their having only one loaf of bread with them? It is so obvious that their minds had not been renewed.

But what about us? Are there times that we have the same type of responses and *reason* with God? (It is okay to take a few moments along the way to repent for doubt and unbelief. Go ahead and take some time to examine your own heart. Grab your pen or highlighter, or dog-ear this page. Remember, when we repent, it renews our minds to comprehend truth.)

Moving on (when you are ready, of course), I want you to picture this for a moment. The disciples had just witnessed a miracle—happening through them—when feeding the thousands. Yet when Jesus brought up leaven and they reasoned with their minds, their attention went to "lack." After all, you can practically hear them thinking: *There is only one loaf and a boat full of people—surely this is what Jesus is referring to.* Lack attempts to dictate our future and rob us of blessings. Lack causes us to focus on what we do not have and limits the power of God in our lives.

Jesus warned the disciples concerning "leaven"—specifically, the leaven of the Pharisees and the leaven of Herod. The disciples missed the point. In the natural, we know that a little leaven spreads out through the dough and causes it to rise. One definition I found described *leaven* as something that not only "lightens" but also "modifies." Without leaven, the bread would look different; it would never rise.

The leaven of the Pharisees is when religion attempts to modify God's Word. Pharisaism today waters down the Gospel, especially any mention of signs, wonders and miracles. Pharisaism is form without power, and Pharisee leaven permeates our minds and limits our perception of the raw power of God. Pharisees also provide many explanations and theories, but not solutions. Have you ever heard a five-step message and when you climbed those steps, there was no change? This is an example of form without power. Plus, Pharisaism blocks repentance and the renewing of the mind, for the evil spirit behind it tells the Pharisees that the knowledge is already within. There is no need to change, the voice says, for they already *know it all.*

The leaven of Herod represents government and dictatorship. It is atheistic in nature. It explains away the miraculous works of Jesus. Bottom line, concerning the leaven of Herod, it most often manifests in the fear of man. When we fear man more than God, our relationship with God becomes modified. Soon we are compromising our calling, ignoring God's directives and negating the anointing on our lives. The pride of man is a state of a puffed-up opinion of self—and the spirit of intellectualism, like leaven, causes this inflated state of ungodly *self*-worth to rise within us.

Dear one, there will always be pressure to follow man rather than God. I know this firsthand, as I was a die-hard "people pleaser" most of my life. Our complete dependence upon God's grace will empower us to remain holy as He is holy. It is also His grace that guides us as we experience His power on earth.

An *unrenewed mind* will always revert to human reasoning, and especially the humanistic reasoning that we are holy due to our own works rather than the finished work of Christ. This is why our minds must be renewed to the truths that involve the Kingdom of heaven. Remember, Jesus brought His world into ours. His desire was to teach the disciples how to bring heaven to earth. He warned them of the leaven that spreads and "modifies" their perception of the dominion available to them. There is limitless power available to us as we demonstrate the Kingdom of God, but they could not comprehend it.

The War in the Mind

Renewing the mind is warfare. The enemy will always attempt to negate the miraculous and try to cause you to doubt the Word of God. Sadly many of us have agreed with what the enemy has said concerning our lives, our ministries and our identities—and there is power in agreement. When we agree with what God says, we are empowered with grace to become more like Him. By the same token, agreeing with the enemy empowers him and robs us of our dominion.

Whenever we walk in the supernatural miraculous power of God, we alert the camp of the enemy—and Satan is ready to send demons to distract us from our anointing. He will bring confusion into the situation, and try to hinder our understanding of the miracle power in us. Remember, Jesus gave us His authority "over all the power of the enemy" (Luke 10:19). As a believer submitted to God, you have the power to resist the devil, and when you do he has to flee from you (see James 4:7). Satan knows he was defeated at the cross, he knows that his power is inferior to the miracle-working power of Jesus within believers. But his trick is to cause us to believe that we are inferior.

This is why so many believers battle inferiority. It is a lie; do not receive it. When you begin to feel inferior, remind yourself of who you are in Christ. Study every Scripture that describes your identity in Christ. Then take some time to examine any area where you have agreed with the lies of the enemy. (We will spend some time on this at the end of this chapter.) This is an important way of renewing your mind.

I am being repetitive on purpose as I write that Jesus brought His world into ours to introduce the Kingdom to us. I repeat it so that you are reminded again that you are a King's kid, appointed and anointed by Him to demonstrate His power on earth. It is up to us to rise up as sons and daughters of our King and possess our rightful inheritance. My heart's desire is for you to break through your limitations so that you experience His power. In a later chapter, I discuss how Jesus visited me and spoke to me of the importance of renewing my mind so that this could take place in me. Precious reader, you have been chosen by the Holy Spirit to have this particular book in your hands. God is renewing your mind with the purpose of transforming you.

> And do not be conformed to this world, but be transformed by the renewing of your mind, that you may prove what is that good and acceptable and perfect will of God.
>
> Romans 12:2 NKJV

I discussed repentance briefly before, but please allow me now to share something I have learned about the action of repenting before God. In all actuality, when I repent, I am reminded that my actions and thoughts have not been aligned with heaven. This causes me to talk more to God about His empowering me with His divine grace to change and align me with heaven's directives. There is no condemnation involved at all—just renewed willingness to be in agreement with Him. Guilt keeps us aligned with the enemy; we each need to understand our freedom in order to be aligned with Kingdom dominion and power over the lies of Satan.

Again, put simply, repentance means to *change the way you think.* Growing up in a strict denominational church, I always attached repentance to shame. When I sinned, I would run back to the altar on Sunday mornings feeling shameful and full of guilt, never fully receiving the grace to change. I believed God was angry with me, and because of His anger toward my sin, I also believed that I deserved to be punished. This is wrong thinking—totally wrong. This is why my mind had to be renewed. I now know that God's wrath toward sin was satisfied at the cross. I am righteous not because of what *I do*, but rather because of who I am in Him and what *He did* at the cross.

God does not desire that we connect the dots of shame, blame, sin and punishment and end up with a picture of defeat. The dots we should connect outline the Kingdom. If we focus on connecting truths (those godly dots along the way), we will notice our minds being renewed and our hearts being softened as we are being transformed more into His image.

A simple example here would be when your heart convicts you that you have sinned. You can believe that when you received Jesus as your Savior—when you realized you needed a Savior, came to Him, asked forgiveness for your sins and were born again—that sin you just committed was also forgiven. Now when we sin, rather than running *from* God we run to Him—with no shame—and repent. If you connect the dots of salvation, redemption, forgiveness and repentance, you have a completed picture of the grace and mercy of God.

I have heard repentance preached like this and I have since ministered it the same way. *Re* means to "go back." That makes sense, right? Go back and rethink the situation and change your mind. This involves aligning your thoughts and your beliefs with what God says. But look at the word again. Think of *re-pent* as *re*-turning to the *pent*-house—a deluxe apartment at the top of a tall building. Looking out from that penthouse you can see things from a much grander perspective—God's view on the situation. Wow! When we repent, we are changing the way we think and aligning ourselves with God's view and His Kingdom perspective on the matters at hand. Actually, this is another way that we *understand* the messages of the Kingdom that Jesus taught.

Be Not Conformed to this World

I have come to the realization that many of us as preachers and leaders have misinterpreted what Jesus meant when He said not to be conformed to this world, but to be transformed by renewing the mind. Many of us have become accustomed to the idea that conforming to the world means avoiding areas that lead us to sin. The problem with this comes with some of the things preachers label as "sin." Watching anything on devil-vision—I mean television—is a big one. And I have actually been rebuked for saying "deviled eggs" rather than "angel eggs." Same with "deviled ham." This ridiculous notion shows how we can become tied to religious performance and legalism.

Being transformed happens from the inside out. Again, when we are saved, we become God's tabernacle—He lives inside us and, therefore, transforms us from the inside. Yes, we become the Governor's mansion. We are His ambassadors on this earth, and His government is never-ending, always and always increasing (see Isaiah 9:6). We, therefore, as believers, should also be increasing in governmental power on earth—moving forth with even more power and demonstration.

The Law and religious works, unlike transformation, affect us (in an ungodly fashion) from the outside in. If our minds are not renewed, we will allow this to happen—neglecting the fact that we are dead to the Law and religious works because Christ became our ultimate sacrifice.

Deuteronomy 28 gives us a hefty list of curses that will come to those who try to keep the Law and fail. But listen to this: The curses listed in that chapter are under the Law, but the blessings are not. When Jesus went to the cross, all the dos and do nots were dealt with. Since Jesus fulfilled the Law, fully and completely, we can simply rebuke the lies of the devil that try to hold us captive to the Law, and then embrace nothing but the blessings attached to the Law. Now, of course, there will be times that we need personal or corporate deliverance to break curses off of repentant believers who opened the door to the enemy. Our focus, though, remains on the finished work of Christ. Jesus stated that deliverance is the children's bread; therefore, I want to be completely free of any demonic oppression as His chosen child.

When we realize not only that He lives in us, but also that we are no longer under the Law and religious performance, nothing can hold us back from experiencing His power in a more dynamic way. Knowing we are the redeemed, and suffer no condemnation, we realize there is nothing impossible to us as we fulfill the divine commission: raising the dead, casting out devils and healing the sick.

On Assignment

Each of us is here on assignment—Kingdom assignment. In Matthew 16:19, Jesus refers to the keys of the Kingdom of heaven:

I will give you the keys of the kingdom of heaven; and whatever you bind (declare to be improper and unlawful) on earth must be what is already bound in heaven; and whatever you loose (declare lawful) on earth must be what is already loosed in heaven.

Matthew 16:19 AMPLIFIED

Keep in mind that Isaiah 22:22 speaks about shutting and opening doors. Believer, use those keys to lock the devil out of your life and to open doors of your promised future.

Listen up again: It is time to use those keys and lock out the enemy and all of his unlawfulness. There is, for instance, no sickness in heaven; therefore, it is unlawful for it to be here on this earth. Whatever was in heaven, Jesus brought with Him to earth. He did not bring sickness with Him. No! He demonstrated heaven by *healing* the sick.

Again, in Matthew 28:18–20, Scripture says that Jesus gave all power and authority to us after His resurrection. It is time to use our authority to recover all that is ours—all that the enemy has stolen from us—and lock the enemy out.

The word *conformed* also means "framed." Examine how you are framed. Do you think as God thinks and truly believe that all things are possible? After all, His Word states that all things are possible to him who believes, right? Or do doubt and unbelief run amuck in your mind?

Dear one, it is time to begin renewing your mind to what God says if your framework does not look like Christ. Many strongholds exist in our thought patterns; it is time to tear down those strongholds as the Word says:

For though we live in the world, we do not wage war as the world does. The weapons we fight with are not the weapons of the world. On the contrary, they have divine power to demolish strongholds. We demolish arguments and every pretension that sets itself up against the knowledge of God, and we take captive every thought to make it obedient to Christ.

2 Corinthians 10:3–5

I define a *stronghold* as "anything that has a *strong hold* on me." If I trust in anything other than God Himself, it will have a strong hold on me. In Greek, a *stronghold* is referred to as something similar to a fortress. I do not desire for Satan to hold me captive in his fortress, do you? Human reasoning will place you in Satan's fortress and lock the cell door tightly behind you. Thank God that our repentance can fling that door open wide.

Food for Thought

Now let's think about the disciples in this process. They had just experienced a great miracle of distributing bread to four thousand people at Jesus' bidding, but we see that the limitation of a hardened heart kept them from truly changing. It is as though He was headed east and the disciples were headed west—that is the simplest way I know to put it. It would be some time before they learned to walk in the limitless power of God.

Believer, we do not have to delay. We can experience God's transforming, miracle-working power within us. To do so, we must pull the plug on powerless traditions and mindsets that harden our hearts; we must remove the leaven of sin. We need God's fresh manna for the seasons ahead.

This will require being in places where you are *hearing*, and *hearing* the Word, so that your faith arises and God can demonstrate His power through you.

He desires to use you to show off. Yes, He wants to demonstrate and show off His glory. The issue really is this: *How much of heaven do you want?* Will you allow Him to demonstrate heaven through you? I believe you will.

Time for Reflection

1. Using the keys of the Kingdom from Matthew 16:19, write below what areas in your life need to be addressed.

   _____

   _____

   _____

2. Take a few moments and examine your thought patterns. Are there any lies of the enemy with which you have agreed? Write them below.

   _____

   _____

   _____

3. Now, precious one, take some time to repent for agreements made with the enemy. Write your repentance prayer below.

   _____

   _____

   _____

4. Think of repentance as going to a penthouse view. How does God view your situation? Receive right now His forgiveness and His grace, which change a hardened heart. Write down the encouraging words that you hear Him saying to you. (This could be a simple thought; maybe you see a picture and you can describe it below, or maybe you hear a certain biblical passage you can write down.)

_____

_____

_____

5. Jesus has given you all power and authority over the enemy. It is important that you act soon whenever you are inspired. This is an indication that you _understand_ what the Spirit of God has instructed. What are you already planning to do—really soon—to help you understand that your heart is changed? Pray for someone? Phone someone to offer encouragement? Write down your action plan below.

_____

_____

_____

9

Power of the Tongue

Letting Go of Disappointments

Take a few moments to examine your life. Go ahead, look around you. Now stop and think about how much of the world around you was shaped and changed by your own mouth. Yes, that is correct. Though difficult to believe, our words have great impact on our world. Look at this Old Testament verse and rediscover just how powerful the tongue is: "Death and life are in the power of the tongue, and those who love it will eat its fruit" (Proverbs 18:21 NASB).

With our tongues (I use the word *mouth* interchangeably), we have a divine ability to make declarations that build up, but also tear down. Obviously, this type of power will affect our living quarters! To understand fully the power of a declaration, I believe we are helped by a brief look at the life of Jeremiah. In this chapter we will observe his call and mandate. We will take portions of Jeremiah 1 in sections so that we can see clearly how the limitation of disappointment keeps us from speaking in power.

Here is the Scripture that we will focus on. The Lord revealed to Jeremiah that four steps were involved in his transformation: "The word of the LORD came to me, saying, 'Before I formed you in the womb I knew you, before you were born I set you apart; I appointed you as a prophet to the nations'" (Jeremiah 1:4–5).

First Step: Formation

The first step involves *formation*. Notice that before Jeremiah was even *formed* in the womb God *knew* him. Before he was even born, he was set apart and *appointed* as a prophet to the nations.

The Hebrew word for *formed* is *yatsar* (pronounced yaw-*tsar*) and it means to "squeeze as into shape, to fashion and to frame." *Strong's* concordance makes mention of the "potter" and how he "molds into shape." The word *purpose* is also mentioned as part of the shaping.

I believe it is safe to say, therefore, that before Jeremiah was in his mother's womb, God took His time as the Potter specifically molding Jeremiah's life with purpose and destiny. In this passage, when God says He *knew* Jeremiah before the womb, He was saying that He had an intimate relationship with him, spending time fashioning and framing Jeremiah's destiny. Is that not amazing?

Allow me to ask you a question. Is Jeremiah any different from any one of us? Is he any different from you? I believe that each of us knew intimacy with God before we were in our mothers' wombs. (We will talk more about intimacy with God in the next chapter.) God fashioned, shaped, framed and molded our potential and destiny together so that we have the opportunity to achieve our purposes on this earth. If God took specific time to mold and shape Jeremiah's future, it only makes sense that He has done the same with each of us.

Now, I can hear some of you saying, "But Jeremiah was called and set apart to be a prophet, one who would declare God's Word. He was special." Dear one, remember: Not all are called to be prophets, but all are called to be what I refer to as a *prophetic people*. *Prophetic people* are those of us (all of us, actually) who know the voice of God, hear the voice of God and follow the voice of God. No one is excluded!

If you have shied away from attempting to hear the voice of God *yourself*, you will likely begin to feel a nudging of the Holy Spirit right about now. This is because God wants to talk to you Himself. Though He has given us prophets, pastors, teachers, evangelists and apostles to share the mind and heart of God, these giftings within the Body were never meant to replace the intimate, personal relationship each of us can have with Him.

In fact, if you are not hearing His voice, you will live a life void of His power. We experience His power—it becomes demonstrated through us—as we determine to remain in intimate relationship with Him. Intimate relationship empowers us with His divine love, and it is love that cultivates greater faith in God. Let me put it this way; this is how He explained it to me personally:

Intimate relationship empowers us with His love. It is a culture of love in which great faith grows. Power and demonstration are the result of the love of God expressed to the children of God whom He loves.

Hearing God's voice is an absolute necessity to demonstrating His power on the earth. Once we *hear* what He is speaking, then it is time to begin to *declare* what He says. It is the *declaring* that begins to shape our environment, rock our world, change our culture—all forms of demonstration and power.

According to *Strong's*, the word *yatsar* is linked to a root word meaning to "press." It is connected to words described as "be distressed, be narrowed, be straitened (in straits) and be vexed." These definitions will give us an entirely new jumping-off point later, but keep this in the back of your mind: Bringing forth God's power and demonstration requires that we go through a "narrow" place and that we experience a "straightened-out place."

When God told Jeremiah that He was appointed, this means that God had set before Jeremiah many godly "appointments." Yes, his destiny was being shaped, formed and fashioned. And like earthly appointments, divine appointments in his future were meant to be kept on time.

It seems to me that every appointment has its own *womb of potential*. Either we show up for the appointment or not—depending upon whether or not we remain on God's timetable, right? And if we miss an appointment? Please also take note of this important fact: *We cannot allow our disappointments to keep us from our divine appointments.* We could camp out there a bit, but we will not take time to discuss our individual disappointments right now. Jeremiah had his own disappointments, which merits study time. And he was hesitant even to get started. Observe the next few verses:

"Ah, Sovereign LORD," I said, "I do not know how to speak; I am only a child." But the LORD said to me, "Do not say, 'I am only a child.' You must go to everyone I send you to and say whatever I command you. Do not be afraid of them, for I am with you and will rescue you," declares the LORD.

Jeremiah 1:6–8

Second Step: Assurance for the Unknown

The second step involves Jeremiah's fears: "I do not know. . . ." Wow! That is something with which we can all identify. Uncertainty about the future robs us of the joy we have today. If we focus on the *I don't knows* we will never fulfill our potential and destiny in God. In fact, the purpose of our being molded, formed, fashioned and set apart in the first place could actually be aborted if we get hung up in the uncertainties of life.

Let's face it: We are not going to know *everything* about our lives. I hear so many people say, "I just want to know the will of God for my life." And they get stuck because they believe that the will of God is some mystical revelation delivered only by an angelic visitation or the audible voice of God. Yet, it is really quite simple. The will of God is expressed clearly in the words Jesus taught the disciples to pray. He said, "Thy will be done on earth as it is in heaven." Dear one, God's will for your life is clear: Just demonstrate heaven on earth. I have mentioned, for instance, that I tell people there is no sickness in heaven; therefore, it does not belong on earth. Then, I allow the Holy Spirit to use me to demonstrate His love by releasing the miraculous. Since

I have learned this heavenly truth, I have witnessed many, many healing miracles—it has been amazing.

Let's examine Jeremiah's response to his calling. Notice that as soon as God told him he would be a prophet, Jeremiah, like Moses, focused on his inability to speak well. He said (and this is my paraphrasing): "God, can't You see that I don't talk well? I'm not a good enough preacher; who would want to listen to someone as young as I am?" (I do not think Jeremiah was referring to his natural age in his response, but rather his lack of maturity.) Can you see here that Jeremiah might have been "dis-appointed" in his ability?

As I stated earlier, disappointment in ourselves—whatever the disappointment might be—can cause us to miss our godly appointments. Note how God responded to Jeremiah. Basically, He said, "Jeremiah, don't say that. You *must* go and you *must* say whatever I command you." Wow! A *must* from God is a weighty command. *Must* in Hebrew is connected to the word *yalak* (pronounced yaw-*lak*), a root word meaning "to walk with a cause, to carry." When I read that translation, I could see immediately a mantle of authority upon Jeremiah's life. His walk in God carried a "cause" with it. In other words, as Jeremiah remained obedient, God would "cause" a reaction to His words as Jeremiah proclaimed them. It was as if every word of God carried potential, and all ears that received those words— the people who truly heard God's plan—would move into their destinies.

It is sad that God's children chose not to listen to Jeremiah's words—but that does not negate the potential of every word he spoke for God. Imagine what might have occurred if they had actually heeded God's warnings and commandments. (We can learn from this ourselves: Let's heed God's Word. There is potential just waiting to be released in our lives.)

Whenever we discuss the *glory* of God, we are also expressing the *weightiness* that His glory "carries" with it. Jesus said that if He revealed all the *mysteries* while on earth, those who heard would not be able to endure. This meant the *weight* of the revelation attached to the hidden mysteries would destroy them if heard all at once. But, precious one, we are living in an hour where mysteries are being revealed. Let's be determined to go where He says and say what He has placed within our mouths so that as we declare His Word, His purposes are fulfilled on earth.

God also told Jeremiah not to fear. Many of us fear the unknown, but God promised Jeremiah that He would protect him in times of uncertainty. Believer, for us to carry the weight of His glory in this season, we must continue to trust God. When the enemy of persecution pops up, God promises to rescue us. Our God is the best at rescuing us, would you not agree? If He can prepare a banquet table for us in the presence of our enemies, it is nothing for Him to rescue us from troubles. Let your faith arise—God cares for you. He is a good, good God. And remember, every time He speaks He is releasing divine potential for us to be empowered.

Now let's examine a few more verses:

> Then the LORD reached out his hand and touched my mouth and said to me, "Now, I have put my words in your mouth. See, today I appoint you over nations and

kingdoms to uproot and tear down, to destroy and over-throw, to build and to plant."

Jeremiah 1:9–10

Third Step: "Touching" the Mouth

God had to "touch" Jeremiah's mouth to appoint him over nations and kingdoms. This is a great place to stop and examine just exactly what God did to Jeremiah in this divine "touch." This word *touch* is the Hebrew word *naga* (pronounced naw-*gah*), which is a root word implying a supernatural grace to fulfill what is needed. I love that, don't you? It means that when God touches us, He is also giving us supernatural grace to accomplish our destiny.

This word gives us further insight. It means "to reach violently, to strike, to punish, to destroy, to cast down, to defeat"—and you know me: I go for the jugular when it comes to destroying any plans of the enemy.

So, with this in mind, we see that when God touched Jeremiah, He was imparting His grace so that Jeremiah could prophetically proclaim His perfect will, but also God was touching or smiting that area of disappointment that Jeremiah had—his disappointment that he could not speak well, the confidence he lacked in his own abilities. Dear one, the enemy will lie to each of us and try to stifle our ability in God. He loves to convince us that we are not carriers of His glory and power. If we believe that lie, we will cower instead of demonstrating the Kingdom of God on this earth.

So, just as God touched Jeremiah's disappointments, He can right now, at this very second, touch your area of weakness. He is ready to smite the enemy, silencing the voice that questions your abilities and striking violently every devil that attempts to exalt itself above the power of God. Go ahead, think on it a minute. Imagine God's hand touching your unbelief, your insecurity, your weaknesses. Now imagine God doing warfare against your enemy; Satan was defeated at the cross. Now stand up and declare to your enemy boldly that nothing—absolutely nothing—will hinder you from fulfilling your potential.

Look again at what God intended for Jeremiah to do with his words—the power of his tongue: "See, today I appoint you over nations and kingdoms to uproot and tear down, to destroy and overthrow, to build and to plant" (Jeremiah 1:10). Yes, with your tongue (your mouth) you also can uproot and tear down, destroy and overthrow, build and plant. Talk about shaping your environment with words! See what power is available to us as we speak.

We have been appointed to tear down the kingdoms of this world, destroy powers of darkness and overthrow thrones of iniquity. And also, we have the power in our words to plant Kingdom seeds that will yield a hundredfold crop of blessing, prosperity, healing, power—the demonstration of God's Kingdom on earth.

Now it is time to examine the last few verses that I wish to discuss concerning Jeremiah's call and destiny:

> The word of the LORD came to me: "What do you see, Jeremiah?" "I see the branch of an almond tree," I replied. The LORD said to me, "You have seen correctly, for I am watching to see that my word is fulfilled."
>
> Jeremiah 1:11–12

Fourth Step: Seeing Your New Season

Notice that in verses 10–11 God asked Jeremiah what he saw. Jeremiah could not see his future until God "touched him." I love the fact that God imparts the ability to "see" as He destroys our enemies and imparts divine grace. So often the enemy blinds us to our potential. But after God touched Jeremiah, he could envision the branch of an almond tree. Dear one, the almond tree is the first tree to bloom in a new season. In other words, Jeremiah saw his future, his new season. No longer would disappointment dictate his steps. God addressed Jeremiah's past disappointment by touching his mouth and, by doing so, judged the disappointment (not Jeremiah).

Finally, Jeremiah could see correctly; he saw his new appointments in God. Jeremiah was able to envision his future properly. Dear one, you can do the same. Start by meditating on the Word of God concerning your own future. As you meditate you can visualize your potential being realized.

After Jeremiah could see correctly, God then promised to watch over His words spoken to Jeremiah to ensure that everything was fulfilled. Dear one, God is doing the very same for each of us. He is touching every weakness, disappointment and area of unbelief, and He is smiting every lie of the enemy attached to it. It is time to see the branch of *your* almond tree budding.

Watching Our Words

Now that we know the power we have in our tongues, we need to heed what we say. And, precious believer, do you realize that your tongue is attached to your heart? Yes! Supernatural things happen when you speak.

Mark 11:14 gives us the example of the power of Jesus' words as He spoke to a fig tree that had no fruit. Actually, all He said was, "May no one ever eat fruit from you again." The next morning, when Jesus and His disciples saw the fig tree, "Peter remembered and said to Jesus, 'Rabbi, look! The fig tree you cursed has withered!'" Peter noted that the tree had been cursed—and that it had died from the roots up. A curse is nothing more than a spoken negative. Now, maybe you are beginning to better understand how we can shape our world with the power in our tongues.

The wicked use this knowledge of cursing to destroy. Proverbs 11 states that a city is overthrown by the mouth of the wicked:

> When it goes well with the [uncompromisingly] righteous, the city rejoices, but when the wicked perish, there are shouts of joy. By the blessing of the influence of the upright and God's favor [because of them] the city is exalted, but it is overthrown by the *mouth* of the wicked.
>
> Proverbs 11:10–11 AMPLIFIED (emphasis added)

Negative things that are said to us can affect our hearts. The only way out is to speak what God says positively about the situation. Take this example. When Satan, the accuser, lies to you and says that God will not provide for you, your immediate response is to declare that God is Jehovah Jireh, your Provider. Or suppose you get sick and the enemy declares that you are going to die. Your response should be to declare boldly that the life of God is in You because He lives in you. We must realize the dynamic power that occurs as we speak. Remember, words will either build up or tear down. We need to learn to speak God's words in every situation.

When We Are Part of the Problem

Throughout life, we are going to face problems and situations over which we have no control. It is important to understand, however, that there are times that we, individually, are at fault and must take responsibility for our disappointments. That enables God to touch and heal that area. As long as we do not take responsibility for our faults, we remain in the old familiar pattern of iniquity and never experience God's power. Why is that? It is because we are choosing not to control our tongues—and this usually happens if we feel someone has wounded, betrayed or spoken evil against us.

Does an unpleasant situation keep recurring in your life? The real question becomes, Have you admitted that maybe you are a common denominator in these instances? Sometimes we forfeit the power to create a new environment with our tongues because our tongues have wagged too much with evil words about others. Ouch! I know this hurts.

If we do not accept responsibility, we are undoubtedly placing blame on someone else. Blame opens doors to our shame, and shame voids us of power. Accepting that we are part of the problem brings healing—and releases God's grace and power. It is important to remember, though, that we cannot change ourselves. We must depend on God's grace to empower us to change as we walk in obedience. Healing and restoration come from complete dependence on Him and not our own strength.

Incurring Judgment

The book of James mentions people who blamed each other and also blamed God. It is clear that these people did not understand the ability to receive God's grace and embrace His divine love.

James 1:13–15 makes quite clear that we are not to say our temptations are from God:

> When tempted, no one should say, "God is tempting me." For God cannot be tempted by evil, nor does he tempt anyone; but each one is tempted when, by his own evil desire, he is dragged away and enticed. Then, after desire has conceived, it gives birth to sin; and sin, when it is full-grown, gives birth to death.

God is not causing our problems. But God *has* provided deliberate solutions for all of them, as you will read.

James 3 speaks of teachers (leaders) and mentions that they receive greater judgment—but not from God: from others judging them. If you are going to be in ministry, whether in the pulpit or the marketplace, you will have judgments come against you. You will be criticized—and criticism hurts. But to live an unfruitful life hurts more. Usually we are criticized because we have "offended" someone. The word *offend* is the Greek word *skandalizo* (pronounced skan-dl-*id*-zo). Two of its meanings are "to entrap" and "to trip up," thus causing one to fall away or to sin. The main word we associate with this is *stumbling block*.

I have read that this idea came into use when cruel people would deliberately place a large block of wood or a large stone (any obstacle, actually) in front of a blind person and then laugh as the individual stumbled and fell. Cruelty like this truly bothers me. Yet it hits close to home.

How often have I heedlessly "offended" someone? When that happens that person is actually "stumbling" over something that could cause a fall. Thinking on this reminds me of the danger of becoming "offended" and challenges me never to do anything purely with the intention of tripping or "offending" another. Particularly as a leader and teacher in the Body of Christ, I need to be cautious, as I would never want someone to fall away from his faith or to stumble because of my selfish actions.

Yet let's look at James 3 and read how it is inevitable that we very human leaders *will* offend:

> Not many [of you] should become teachers (self-constituted censors and reprovers of others), my brethren, for you know that we [teachers] will be *judged* by a higher standard and with greater severity [than other people; thus we assume the greater accountability and the more condemnation].
>
> For we all often *stumble and fall and offend* in many things. And if anyone does not offend in speech [never says the wrong things], he is a fully developed character and a perfect man, able to control his whole body and to curb his entire nature.
>
> If we set bits in the horses' mouths to make them obey us, we can turn their whole bodies about. Likewise, look at the ships: though they are so great and are driven by rough winds, they are steered by a very small rudder wherever the impulse of the helmsman determines.
>
> Even so the tongue is a little member, and it can boast of great things. See how much wood or how great a forest a tiny spark can set ablaze! And the tongue is a fire. [The tongue is a] world of wickedness set among our members,

contaminating and depraving the whole body and setting on fire the wheel of birth (the cycle of man's nature), being itself ignited by hell (Gehenna).

For every kind of beast and bird, of reptile and sea animal, can be tamed and has been tamed by human genius (nature). But the human tongue can be tamed by no man. It is a restless (undisciplined, irreconcilable) evil, full of deadly poison. With it we bless the Lord and Father, and with it we curse men who were made in God's likeness! Out of the same mouth come forth blessing and cursing. These things, my brethren, ought not to be so.

Does a fountain send forth [simultaneously] from the same opening fresh water and bitter? Can a fig tree, my brethren, bear olives, or a grapevine figs? Neither can a salt spring furnish fresh water.

James 3:1–12 AMPLIFIED

Dear believer, we have discussed the good, bad and evil of the tongue. We have discussed that it is time to enter a new season of power and demonstration. Also, we discussed how the tongue is equipped to curse and speak evil things that cause barrenness and an unfruitful life. We have studied how our words can offend others and cause them to stumble. Now it is time for self-reflection.

Time for Reflection

It is time to ask the Holy Spirit, the Teacher of truth, to speak to your heart concerning the limitation of disappointments and the power of the tongue when used in obedience to God's plan for our lives. Allow me to lead you in prayer as you enter into His divine presence:

Father God, I have come to the place of understanding that I have the divine ability to shape and change my world. Like Jeremiah, I recognize my disappointments and weaknesses, yet I know that You have touched me in a mighty way. It is time to enter a new season. Holy Spirit, come now, and show me areas in which I need to see and understand so that I can be transformed more into the likeness of Jesus. In His name, Amen.

1. Take a minute to examine your life. Again, ask the Holy Spirit to speak to you concerning this time of personal reflection. Does anything come to mind that you have complained about—even if you have given equal time to praying about it? List below your complaint. Then write a positive confession that will negate the complaint and change your environment. In other words, replace negative thoughts with positive thoughts.

I confess this negative thought:

_____

_____

Lord, I ask forgiveness for the negative confession. Now I confess what God says about the situation:

_____

_____

Remember, what we complain about gets stronger and stronger until it becomes so magnified we cannot find a way to conquer it. Words of righteousness, however, will deliver us.

2. List the ways in which you can relate to Jeremiah. Ask yourself if you have been disappointed in the past. If so, write those disappointments below as well.

_____

_____

_____

Now, find Scriptures that declare what God says concerning your disappointment or weakness (or any area in which you have related to Jeremiah that hinders your faith in God and limits your abilities). Write them below. After writing them down, stand up and declare boldly what God says. This will change your atmosphere. Try to do this every day until it becomes a reality—and then still keep doing it.

Keep in mind that your declaration must become a part of your belief system. Declaring a truth that never is birthed in your heart as the truth could easily become legalistic action. We will learn in the next chapter that intimacy with God is vital for God's power to transform your life. As you draw closer to Him, you will realize His desire for you to be transformed as well as His desire to release His power through the words that you proclaim. Along with this incredible power is divine grace to continue to speak His Word in faith.

All of this self-reflection is *not* to make us focused on our lack but to open the eyes of our hearts, to see and walk in truth and depend fully upon His grace for transformation and power.

---

3. What would you like for your new season to look like or involve? Believer, God wants to give His good gifts to you. He wants you to "see" your new season. Write below what you see as His purpose for you—your heart's true desire. Again, after writing it down, stand up and decree your new season while keeping in mind that this is not a ritual or legalistic program. After decreeing God's truth concerning your new season, also speak aloud boldly and decree that God is watching over your new season to see it come to pass. Yes, He is the Watchman on the wall of your life. What He declares concerning you will happen!

10

Hungering for More of His Presence

Letting Go of Fear of Intimacy with God

There is absolutely nothing that compares. I am referring to the presence of the Lord. This chapter is written for the sole purpose of helping you let go of the fear of intimacy and develop passion for the presence of God. And, more particularly, since this book is about experiencing the power of God and demonstrating it on earth, I want you to understand that this occurs as "normal Christian life"—demonstrating His Kingdom is often a result of spending time in His presence.

I so desire for you to hunger to see God face to face. You might have been taught that no one can see Him face to face. It is true that when Moses cried out to see God's glory, He hid Moses in a rock because no man could see His face and live. I write more on that in a bit. For now, realize this important fact: We, as New Testament believers, being born again in Christ, are able to "behold Him as He is." This actually empowers us to see His face.

Now, I am not referring to seeing Him with natural eyes, but with eyes of the Spirit. And, quite frankly, as I let go of my fears of this kind of intimacy, I began to experience effortlessly what I used to strive so hard to achieve in my own strength: witnessing miracles, signs and wonders. I can hear you asking a question: Why is that so? Well, it is because when His glory is present, we see transformation occur in and through our lives simply because His presence rests on us. (More on that later, too.)

Dear one, take heed: I am giving you wisdom and revelation that took me years to understand. This is not simply for Sandie Freed! No, it is also for you. It is God's plan that a testimony be realized within every person and every generation. If you recall, *testimony* means "Do it again, God." So when I write and share revelation and give testimony to His desires, His divine nature and who He really is, you have an immediate opportunity (upon receiving revelation God gives you) to repent and change any wrong ways you think—about God *and* yourself.

Please lock into this understanding now. This is not about following a formula or working in your own strength. All that God desires for your life—your future, your potential for intimacy with Him—was accomplished when Jesus Christ died for you and me. The power of the blood of Jesus will defeat the accuser when he attempts to nullify your value and worth. You may even believe you are not "qualified" to demonstrate and experience God's power. In my recent book, *The Power in the Blood: Claiming Your Spiritual Inheritance* (Chosen, 2012), you can read *how* to apply His blood for victory. But, for now, please know with certainty that God wants you to experience so much more of His presence and His power.

I have learned that I can be content and satisfied by Him *daily* just by spending time in His presence. And each time I put Him first in my life I desire even more of Him. It is true that there is sacrifice involved—putting aside my personal desires when I would like to enjoy some "couch time," for instance. But I can say with confidence that what I give of myself to obtain more of Him is a really good deal. I am through with *status quo*. By the time you finish reading this chapter, I think you will be in agreement—and you will realize it is something you can do (you can spend more time with God so that you can truly *know Him*). So keep reading—you will not be disappointed.

The apostle Paul's prayer is being answered today. He writes, "[I] give thanks for you, making mention of you in my prayers; that the God of our Lord Jesus Christ, the Father of glory, may give to you the spirit of wisdom and of revelation in the knowledge of Him" (Ephesians 1:16–17 NKJV). It is this author's belief that as we gain revelation about and knowledge of Jesus, we begin to see Him as He is—we actually see Him face-to-face. Actually, the word "face" is the Greek word *prosopon* (pronounced *pros*-o-pon) and it not only translates as "countenance and appearance," but it goes further to mention the word "presence." So, I believe we can safely conclude that when we are in His divine *presence,* we are also seeing Him face to face. How awesome is that thought?

Are you excited about this revelation? I believe that you are as hungry for more of His presence as I am. Keep in mind that He says, "I will never leave you or forsake you." That means that He is *always* with us. But we are still encouraged in the Word to "seek Him" and to spend time "meditating" on His Word and His teachings. Again, this is not legalism or a proven program that you have to adhere to. It is really simple. Just take some time to talk to Him, and then listen with your heart to what is on His heart.

Everywhere I travel, and even in our own ministry in the Hurst, Texas, area, people are crying out not only to experience God's presence, but also to see Him face to face. Because seeking more of His presence has become all-consuming for me, I can honestly say that I believe this has come with a great price. It was not a price, however, that *you and I* had to pay. Jesus paved the way for intimacy with God when He demonstrated His love at the cross. Our price is simple obedience to seek Him—not because He *demands* it, but because we truly *want* to. When we see ourselves as His *friends* rather than *slaves* or *servants,* we will seek Him out simply because we desire to talk to Him and truly *listen.*

Dear one, I believe that as Christians, we are all in this place—seeking His presence *more.* Why? Well, besides the simple fact that we need His presence, there is also so much uncertainty in the world today. It is difficult to have faith as we encounter so many difficulties. Let's face it: We need Him every day.

Double Straits

While writing this book, traveling and ministering through-out the United States and Canada, I had a dream of Satan's hand. In his hand he was holding a list of assignments—assaults planned against us as believers. Five particular attacks were written down, and I knew in the dream that he was about to pass these plans on to strong territorial ruling spirits and principalities. I was not able to read the last four written there, but the first one, the first planned assault printed there, was this: *double straits.*

I got up immediately to write down the dream because I was certain of two things: The dream was from God and I was being given revelation of how to fight this battle. God wanted me to share with others—and that includes you! I know you want to be prepared and empowered with victory, so read on.

Let's begin with a look at the word *Egyptian.* It translates, of course, as "an inhabitant of Egypt," but oddly enough it also means "double straits." Many theologians tie the idea of double straits to "both sides of the Nile River." What first came to my mind, however, is the fact that the children of Israel were released from their slavery in Egypt to a new life with God, but they were never able to get Egypt out of their hearts—they were double minded. If you will recall, Moses had not even come down from the mountain before they built a false idol dedicated to Baal, one of the principle idols of Egypt. And God spoke numerous times of the Israel-ites' carrying personal idols with them as they journeyed through the wilderness. Even after Joshua led them into the Promised Land, Israel kept committing apostasy. She began worshiping idols again—which led to even more captivity and bondage.

So, I believe that God is still putting His holy finger upon that subject: idolatry. To be at a place of double straits is to be double-minded concerning God. Idolatry is any area in our lives that takes the place of God. Many believers have counterfeit gods and never realize it. I have written about idolatry in several of my books, and God has opened doors through these books that have led many to repentance. *Breaking the Threefold Demonic Cord: Exposing and Defeating Jezebel, Athaliah and Delilah* (Chosen, 2008) exposes how Jezebel brought her idols into Israel and how Athaliah, her daughter, brought the same idols her mother worshiped (maybe even more) into Judah. And I discuss how Delilah was seduced by Mammon (the name of a false Syrian god) to destroy Samson—God's chosen. I wrote *Crushing the Spirits of Greed and Poverty: Defeating the Strongholds of Babylon and Mammon* (Chosen, 2010) concerning Mammon as an idol and how it is strongly connected with the spirit of the world (Babylon). Also, another book that exposes idolatry is entitled *The Jezebel Yoke: Breaking Free from Bondage and Deception* (Chosen, 2012). I tell you this in the event that you would like to read in more detail about how to rid your heart of anything—sports, television, children, mates, jobs—that has become a counterfeit god. No, obviously I am not advocating that you leave your spouse, quit your job or give your children over to an adoption agency! What I mean by this is that you examine your heart and repent—change the way you think. Simply put God first in your life and you will be amazed at the way this will open the door for you to seek His face passionately.

Birth Pangs

The importance of understanding *double straits* does not stop here. Double straits are connected to *birthing* and *birth pangs*. We are in a season when great revelation is being poured out by the Holy Spirit. Like a woman in labor, we are experiencing birth pangs, signaling an imminent delivery. Let's get excited, as greater revelation is coming. Precious believer, the Holy Spirit is unlocking mysteries that have been held up. These revealed mysteries will draw us nearer into His presence—and in His presence He will pour out more of His power for us to demonstrate on earth.

The word *straits* in Hebrew is connected also to words meaning "distress, trouble, narrow and birthing." I am sure you can relate to distressing times; we have all experienced difficulties. I am reminded of Hezekiah when he was under assault. He said this about troubled times (double straits): "Thus saith Hezekiah, This day is a day of *trouble*, and of rebuke, and blasphemy: *for the children are come to the birth, and there is not strength to bring forth*" (2 Kings 19:3 KJV, emphasis added).

Okay. Did you get that? He was in a troubled place (double straits) and it was time to birth, and yet there was no strength to deliver. I am sure you have been aware that the enemy targets the strengths of every believer. In Daniel 7:25, we notice the enemy's plan is to wear out the saints through persecution. Dear believer, the enemy is trying to wear you out so that you are ineffective. How do we battle against this type of assault? We remain in Jesus' presence. We become people in intimate relationship with Him.

The Enemy's Stumbling Blocks

There are numerous ways that the enemy engages in this assault against our seeking intimacy in God's presence, but one seems particularly successful for him. In this attack he wears down believers and takes away our strength for delivery. We discussed in the last chapter the danger of being "offended." This is one of Satan's main areas of warfare. If he can encourage us to become "offended" with life, or sometimes with God, we will pull back—or even fall away. This is a significant block to intimacy.

We recall the cruel practice of placing a block of wood in front of a blind person who would stumble over it, and the perpetrators would then laugh. So what did Jesus mean by telling His disciples that He, Himself, would be a stumbling block to many? He had come with the purpose to die on the cross. His Kingship was not of this world. Many people, however, in anguish over living under Roman occupation, hoped He would become their king and lead them out of oppression. They wanted Him to govern in the natural realm. In other words, Jesus was not fulfilling their expectations of what He should be doing. These people were blinded by their desires. And they "stumbled" over—they were offended by—the Truth in their determination to fulfill their own mission.

And are not many of us the same way? It is possible for any one of us to stumble over present Kingdom manifestation because we become "blinded" by offenses. It is difficult to maintain faith in a world of problems. If we do not guard our hearts, we will look at our circumstances with natural eyesight and stumble over them rather than grow in intimacy with God. This is why we need *more of His presence*—we will be strengthened as we see Him as He is.

His Strength Through Hard Times

For me, the realization for the need of intimacy in His presence was fully realized after my mother died. Fifteen years after her miraculous healing from lung cancer, she succumbed to liver cancer. It was my "double strait" time. My sister, Pam, and I had brought Mother home for hospice care and we were her main caregivers. Never before had I cried out to God in the way that I did as I watched her waste away day after day. Yet, through it all, Mother never gave up hope of being healed. I, on the other hand, was amazed at her great faith.

When I realized that she, a dying person, had more faith than I was demonstrating, I realized I needed a heavenly invasion. I desperately needed heaven to touch my earth, and I needed to see God in this situation, somehow. As a result, I began to write a book: *Heaven's Voice Touching Earth: Hearing the Sounds of Heaven* (Kingdom Word Publishers, 2008). I learned that if I could find peace in His presence, I would be strengthened to face my daily challenges.

One of the ways I know that I am in His presence is when I hear God's voice, so I focused on that manifestation. I had a whole list of questions to talk to God about. Number One was, "Why aren't You healing my mother?" Yet, each day Mother would say, "Sandie, grab your computer and write some more about hearing heaven's voice." She was an active part of the book as she released her faith for me to write, and each day we prayed that both of us would experience more of God's presence.

But this was a "double strait" time for me. I was, on the one hand, praying for her healing, but, on the other hand, expecting her to die. I figured that the Lord was preparing my heart for her to see Him face to face—*in heaven*. This was because I did not see positive changes in her physically, and I was doing the best I could to hold on to what little faith I had left.

She, however, understood intimacy with God. She had no intention of waiting until death to be in His presence. She wanted His presence there with her that minute—right where she was in the house—and not have to die physically in order to have that closeness with Him. Oh, my, what faith and courage Mother had!

I would click away on my computer, writing for hours on end, it seemed. Then I would then take breaks to talk to Mother about her childhood. I wanted memories tanked up so that I could easily recall our time together. We would always end up discussing the goodness of God and how wonderful His presence was. Since she was taking many drugs for pain, she would often slip in and out of consciousnesses. She usually slept with a smile on her face, and I knew beyond a shadow of a doubt that the Holy Spirit was ministering somehow to her. Then I would seek further revelation as to how to hear God's voice—even in the midst of great trials. God was faithful as He poured out revelation regarding touching heaven and bringing God's Kingdom to earth. Hearing His voice and witnessing His divine presence became more and more important to me.

Maybe you have been a caregiver for someone who was ill, or for an elderly parent. Maybe you have a sick child and you are standing firm in prayer for a physical healing. It is important *never* to give up. Do not allow your natural circumstances to rob you of pressing in to His divine presence. Your natural understanding could cause you to become offended and you might stumble and be tempted to fall away. This is not a time to cower from what we see in the natural, but rather to access the unseen with greater faith. It is possible to hear the voice of the Lord, which will encourage you through difficult times. When we hunger for Him, we are encouraged to have great faith in a God who does what appears to be impossible.

The Divine Visitation

Mom went to heaven in September 2007. She is forever in His presence. Though we did not see her healed here on this earth, she is walking the streets of gold with Jesus and having a glorious time. Although I grieved, I did not allow her death to cause me to stumble, but that experience did cause me to hunger and thirst for *more* of Jesus. You, also, in good times and bad can press in, asking Him for *more*—right now. He will be faithful to speak and manifest His presence. Ask God to invade your atmosphere as you spend more time ministering to Him. Ministering *to God* is different from ministering to His people. I need, for instance, to sing songs *to* Him in intimate worship—this will cause His presence to manifest.

It was in February 2009 that I had a divine visitation that radically changed my life. First, let me tell you what I was going through. I was having brain seizures that were puzzling the neurologist. I would lose hours of time, even days, without remembering anything. If you read my book *Silencing the Accuser* (Chosen, 2011), you will remember that while I was in the emergency room after one seizure,

I could not pull my thoughts together. I could focus only on one thing—prayer not to lose my ability to write. Writing is my passion. I recall praying silently to God that He would not allow my mind to be affected in a way that would keep me from writing more about Him and His goodness.

It was another *double strait* time for me. And as it often the case, it involved being *double-minded*. I realize now that when we are in such a narrow place, in double straits, it is difficult to maintain faith. It seemed that one minute I could believe God to heal me and then the next minute fear would overwhelm me. James 1:8 says that "a double-minded man is unstable in all his ways" (KJV). How true this was for me during difficult times—bouncing from faith to fear, feeling completely unstable!

Interestingly, James connects this instability and double-mindedness with resisting the devil:

> Submit yourselves therefore to God. Resist the devil, and he will flee from you. Draw nigh to God, and he will draw nigh to you. Cleanse your hands, ye sinners; and purify your hearts, ye double-minded.
>
> James 4:7–8 KJV

Precious believer, it is clear that our times of being double-minded concerning our faith in God involve "resisting the devil." We must resist the devil, and if we do, God promises us that the enemy has to flee. Notice that James encourages us also to draw close to God (get in His presence as we discussed earlier) and purify our hearts. When we purify our hearts we are ridding our hearts of doubt and unbelief and double-mindedness. Wow! That is amazing warfare strategy.

After the doctor ruled out a stroke, the very first thing on my mind was to grab my computer and begin to write. I was hungering to continue to write and was experiencing much contention from the enemy. Then one night, completely exhausted from the warfare, I cried out for God's presence. I had reached the conclusion that I was the problem in this equation, that I had maybe committed a terrible sin and that was why I was under such demonic assault. Even though I knew that all of my sins were forgiven at the cross, I was so tired and exasperated that I could not think straight. Have you ever felt that way? Read on.

As I prayed to witness His presence and divine intervention, I experienced an incredible supernatural encounter with Jesus Christ. I have dreamed of Him many times, but this was an actual physical manifestation. As I cried out to Him in desperation, suddenly a lightning bolt shot through the room. I saw it with my natural eyes—a brilliant white flash of light. Then a surge of power hit my brain—and for over an hour my head was jerking and bobbing uncontrollably. I knew that it was God, but I could not help but think, *What if this is somehow changing the shape of my head—or my face? Will my eyebrows end up pointed like Mr. Spock's on* Star Trek? (I know. It must have been a woman thing. But I was willing to give up my dignity for an increased measure of His presence and visitation.) Then I heard the voice of Jesus. He spoke with electrifying power. His words to me will always remain at the forefront of my life's quest to seek Him more. Jesus said to me, *Sandie, don't you know I would never leave you or forsake you? There is absolutely* nothing *you could ever do that would cause Me to stop loving you. And when your mind is renewed you will understand how much I love you.*

God's Grace and Love

Within minutes the electrical charge left and I got out of bed to write about the visitation. It has been several years since that night, and I must admit that I have been on a quest ever since for more of His presence and greater understanding of His divine grace. After all, I have always been a performer, and until then I did not understand that to move in divine power, I would be required to do so under His grace. Each day in my prayer time, I keep asking Him for more revelation concerning His goodness and to see Him face to face—and quite often I have reminded the Lord that Moses asked to see His glory and that God honored Moses' request:

> Then Moses said, "Now show me your glory."
> And the LORD said, "I will cause all my goodness to pass in front of you, and I will proclaim my name, the LORD, in your presence. I will have mercy on whom I will have mercy, and I will have compassion on whom I will have compassion. But," he said, "you cannot see my face, for no one may see me and live."
> Then the LORD said, "There is a place near me where you may stand on a rock. When my glory passes by, I will put you in a cleft in the rock and cover you with my hand until I have passed by. Then I will remove my hand and you will see my back; but my face must not be seen."
>
> Exodus 33:18–23

I am convinced that this visitation was a type and shadow of how believers cling to Christ, the Rock. I am excited each time I remind myself that I am "hidden in Christ" (Colossians 3:3). Believer, God is hiding you right now in the cleft of the Rock. The Rock is Jesus Christ, and no matter what you experience, no matter how many hard times you face, no matter how many double straits you endure, you are hidden completely in Christ. And, yes, you will be strong to deliver whatever you have been impregnated with by His Spirit.

But, at the same time, we are seated with Him in heavenly places (see Ephesians 2:6). Because of Him we each represent God's glory on this earth, and this is because of who Christ is in each of us, as Colossians 1:26–27 states: "Even the mystery which hath been hid from ages and from generations, but now is made manifest to his saints: to whom God would make known what is the riches of the glory of this mystery among the Gentiles, *which is Christ in you, the hope of glory*" (KJV, emphasis added).

Be assured that you are protected, loved and provided for. His glory is in you, and you are seated in heavenly places with Him. It is time for you to see yourself as victorious over every situation. As you draw closer and become more intimate with Him, His grace will be there for anything you need. You will move forward, leaving the past behind and possessing every promise.

I hunger to learn more and more about the grace of God and His divine love for me and for those who are willing to co-labor with Him to build His Kingdom. I witnessed His presence in a very tangible way, and this has made me desire even more of Him in my life. Many people are content simply to discuss the presence of God, but many others are willing to pay the price to seek Him daily and truly experience and encounter His presence. You can have this same experience as you let Him calm your fears and begin to hunger for Him.

Time for Reflection

I truly believe with all my heart that God is answering my prayers and times of crying out for *more*. You can ask the same of Him—maybe you can start right now.

Allow me to pray for you:

Father God, I know that it is Your desire to reveal Your divine glory through us who believe. I pray for this reader today that You will draw this one unto Yourself, and that You will begin to reveal Your glory. Lord, I join this reader in crying out for more of Your presence. Without You and Your presence we will never be completely fulfilled. You are all that we need in life to be content. Empower us as we pursue our destinies and the demonstration of Your Kingdom on earth. In Jesus' name, Amen.

Dear one, you are in my heart each day. I have prayed for you in advance and I am grateful to the Lord that you are on this journey with me. It is no accident that you hold this book in your hands. You want to experience His presence and His power on the earth. Up to this point we have loosed Satan's firm grip of legalism and religion. We have pressed past hardships, double straits and times of trouble. You have become strengthened in the Lord and the power of His might. And you are aware that your heart hungers for more intimacy with Him.

Now, let's take a look at one more important aspect of letting go of our limitations. Get ready: We are going to study about the Promised Land called *rest*. We each need to come to this place because the place God promised us is a place of rest. Once we can rest in the finished work of Christ, we are living the promises of God and experiencing the raw power of God in our lives—and experiencing His transforming power.

11

The Promised Land Called Rest

Letting Go of the Don'ts

I know what you might be thinking: *What does entering into our promised land called "rest" have to do with letting go of things that limit me from experiencing God's transforming power?* Well, the answer is, everything! Until we let go of our limitations and stop striving and believing it is up to *us* and our *intellect* and our *performance*, we will diminish God's power flowing through us.

But allow me to warn you that the enemy does not want you to enter into this place of rest. In the last chapter we discussed *double straits*. Two other definitions concerning *double straits* are "bottlenecked" and "choked." Let's look at these words for a moment.

Being Bottlenecked

I have two thoughts to share with you concerning the word *bottlenecked* as it applies to our demonstrating

God's power. First, intellect, human reasoning, selfish ambition and self-*anything* will "bottleneck" the anointing. Believe me, God knows just *how* to address this. He will speak to your heart—and not necessarily through a recognized minister. If you spend quality time with Him, if you *seek His face*, you will respond immediately to the conscience of your own heart. Second, I have also learned that His presence supersedes principles. God desires to break in on us and show us His glory—and that glory rests on us.

It is the anointing that breaks through the bottlenecks of oppression, sickness, disease, depression. We are simply obedient vessels, remaining obedient by grace, demonstrating His power with an anointing to break others free also. It is Christ, the Anointed One, working through obedient vessels empowered by His divine grace that breaks Satan's hold. I love ministering while experiencing the anointing; this is a sure sign of His presence and His "tabernacling" inside of me. And when His presence and glory come, this is a sign that the bottleneck has been broken and He can enter in and find a resting place.

Problem is, we ourselves need to find that promised land of rest so that His glory can rest upon us. This next statement might sound as if I am double-minded as I write—let me assure you that I am not. On the one hand, we keep in mind that, as those *chosen* to carry a burden-removing anointing, we must make the effort to seek intimacy with God. On the other hand, we also recognize that it is not *we* who are working the miraculous. It is never by our own might or power, but by His Spirit. Hang in there; we are going somewhere important in this chapter.

Choked by a Python Spirit

Now consider the word *choked*. I am reminded of how a *python spirit* attempts to choke us, choke the Word out of our spirits right at the point of breakthrough. Let me back up a bit and discuss this evil spirit. I have written numerous times concerning the python spirit that lies in wait on the threshold of our breakthroughs. The apostle Paul speaks of opposition when doors of opportunity are opened to us: "A wide door of opportunity for effectual [service] has opened to me [there, a great and promising one], and [there are] many adversaries" (1 Corinthians 16:9 AMPLIFIED).

As we study the spiritual aspects of the word *threshold*, I believe it is safe to say it forms the bottom of a wide door of opportunity opened to us, the point of entry to a place of great increase. As we hunger for God, seeking increased anointing and power of the Holy Spirit, we are going to have adversaries working against us. Another way of looking at the word *threshold* is to consider going through a "narrow place." We discussed earlier about being at the point of birth with little strength to deliver. And if you recall, *double straits* also means "narrow." So, we can put together this information to help us see that at a time of crossing over to places of increase, we go through a narrow entryway.

Also spiritually symbolic is the idea of a python snake—a snake that kills its victims by squeezing the life from them, "constricting" them. Quite literally, a python can squeeze or "choke" off the breath of its victim. The Greek name for *python* is the *puthon*—which is the word used for *divination*. This is the sprit that Paul encountered while in Greece (see Acts 16:16). Obviously, Paul had a door for effectual service offered to him, but as he crossed the threshold, he encountered a python spirit lying in wait to destroy him. If you recall the story, Paul rebuked the spirit of divination that was working through a slave girl, and, as a result, Silas and he were both thrown into prison.

Why am I discussing this? Because to be forewarned is also to be forearmed. Knowing that an adversary might attempt to destroy us as we labor to enter into rest will keep us focused. Remind yourself who you are in God if the enemy attempts to choke the life out of you, your calling or your destiny. God is opening a door for you to enter into effectual service.

The "*Don't*-eronomies"

Dear one, not only is our promised land a land of milk and honey, it is also a land of resting in God and knowing that He has promised us all good things. The blessings listed in Deuteronomy are a kind of summation of these good things. Christ paid a very high price to give it all to us; He wants us to experience His blessings bought at the cross.

I mentioned this earlier, but want to review it here. Due to so much legalistic preaching (and I have been guilty of this myself), we tend to focus on all of the *don'ts* in the book of Deuteronomy. Since we are no longer under the Law, however, we are no longer cursed. And, further, we still get all the blessings. Legalism seems to refer to "*Do*-teronomy" as "*Don't*-eronomy"! If we remain in the don'ts, we will never move forward and possess our inheritance. These don'ts may sound like this:

- You don't measure up to God's standards; therefore, you will never receive the blessing.

- You don't pray long enough to receive God's best.
- You don't go to church enough. God doesn't bless those who aren't in church at every service.
- You don't visit the sick in the hospital enough, so why should God heal you?

I have to admit that I was one of those who could never find rest. I never felt qualified or good enough to rest in Jesus and His finished work. Until I was in my thirties and began to understand just a little concerning grace, every Sunday I would be at the altar repenting and asking to become "born again" *again*! And, if I didn't make my way to the altar myself, someone who felt more religious than I would grab me and convince me I needed to go up there and repent *once more*—or the preacher would remind me *once more* of my sin. Dear one, with preaching and teaching that condemns continually, we will never enter a promised land of rest.

There were times when I felt I needed to wear my spiritual armor *especially* in church, because it was difficult to get through a service without feeling condemned. (And, believe me, until I fully understood grace, I was one of those preachers who spoke so much on holiness it seemed impossible to ever be holy enough.) I know now—really know—that there is no condemnation in Christ Jesus. I was not told in my earlier years that I was already righteous in Christ, so I kept trying in my own strength to be righteous. Now, if the enemy says that I have messed up, his lies have to bounce back upon him because my heart is protected by my breastplate of righteousness.

Many preachers say to put on the full armor of God every day. My thinking is, *Why ever take it off?* Walk in it all the time so the devil does not have any opportunity to abort your destiny in God. Religion needs to die. Let's not look any longer for rules we must try our best to keep. Rather, let us seek relationship. Our relationship with God is not fear-based; it is all faith-based—and without faith it is impossible to please Him. God has an abundant life planned for you! Simply believe it with childlike faith and you will see the world differently. Instead of focusing on the negative, you will see with God's lenses of hope and joy.

Take some time and read the book of Deuteronomy. As you do, you will notice that we are told to "keep all the commandments." As we know, because of Jesus' sacrifice as the perfect Lamb of God, we are no longer under the Law: The curses promised for non-compliance of the rules were settled at the cross. Then, if you take some time and study Deuteronomy 11:8–32, you will begin to get excited about all the blessings God has for you because Jesus fulfilled the Law perfectly and forever. I will put these verses for you below. Remember as you read that we are not under Old Testament Law, so we can observe the commandments that Jesus gives in the New Testament and by *grace* do as He instructs us in life:

> Observe therefore all the commands I am giving you today, so that you may have the strength to go in and take over the land that you are crossing the Jordan to possess, and so that you may live long in the land that the LORD swore to your forefathers to give to them and their descendants, a land flowing with milk and honey. The land you are entering to take over is not like the land of Egypt, from which you have come, where you planted your seed and irrigated it by foot as in a vegetable garden. But the land you are crossing the Jordan to take possession of is a land of mountains and

valleys that drinks rain from heaven. It is a land the LORD your God cares for; the eyes of the LORD your God are continually on it from the beginning of the year to its end.

So if you faithfully obey the commands I am giving you today—to love the LORD your God and to serve him with all your heart and with all your soul—then I will send rain on your land in its season, both autumn and spring rains, so that you may gather in your grain, new wine and oil. I will provide grass in the fields for your cattle, and you will eat and be satisfied.

Be careful, or you will be enticed to turn away and worship other gods and bow down to them. Then the LORD's anger will burn against you, and he will shut the heavens so that it will not rain and the ground will yield no produce, and you will soon perish from the good land the LORD is giving you. Fix these words of mine in your hearts and minds; tie them as symbols on your hands and bind them on your foreheads. Teach them to your children, talking about them when you sit at home and when you walk along the road, when you lie down and when you get up. Write them on the doorframes of your houses and on your gates, so that your days and the days of your children may be many in the land that the LORD swore to give your forefathers, as many as the days that the heavens are above the earth [days of heaven upon the earth, KJV].

If you carefully observe all these commands I am giving you to follow—to love the LORD your God, to walk in all his ways and to hold fast to him—then the LORD will drive out all these nations before you, and you will dispossess nations larger and stronger than you. Every place where you set your foot will be yours: Your territory will extend from the desert to Lebanon, and from the Euphrates River to the western sea. No man will be able to stand against you. The LORD your God, as he promised you, will put the terror and fear of you on the whole land, wherever you go.

See, I am setting before you today a blessing and a curse—the blessing if you obey the commands of the LORD your God that I am giving you today; the curse if you disobey the commands of the LORD your God and turn from the way that I command you today by following other gods, which you have not known. When the LORD your God has brought you into the land you are entering to possess, you are to proclaim on Mount Gerizim the blessings, and on Mount Ebal the curses. As you know, these mountains are across the Jordan, west of the road, toward the setting sun, near the great trees of Moreh, in the territory of those Canaanites living in the Arabah in the vicinity of Gilgal. You are about to cross the Jordan to enter and take possession of the land the LORD your God is giving you. When you have taken it over and are living there, be sure that you obey all the decrees and laws I am setting before you today.

I love this—especially that I can witness days of heaven on earth.

But if I focus on all of the *If yous*, I know I cannot fulfill them. When we teach the finished work of Christ and the cross, we can stamp this covenant *Paid in full*. Here we are two thousand years later trying to make payment for this covenant when it has been paid in full. The only *If you* we have to worry about is *If you* come to Jesus. We do not have to do any of the *I wills* except *I will* come to Jesus and *I will* be given all of this.

The land of milk and honey. It is time to enter into all of it. This "heaven on earth" is our resting place.

My question to you now is this: *If where you go to church is not like a slice of heaven, do you still want to go there?* There are many "terrorist" preachers (and I may have even been one of them in my earlier years) who try to frighten us into getting holier, more committed and living a better lifestyle. I taught a great deal about sin—in my fervor even condemning makeup. Oh, my, what a religious spirit I had! Nobody there could get qualified to get saved by my standards. Actually, I am thankful for makeup. Ugly does not suit me well. When I started learning how to dress better and use makeup, my husband handed me the credit card and said, "Keep looking good!"

I used to wish I could go back about thirty years and start over. Now I no longer feel condemned. I can run to the Father knowing that I am already forgiven. At the throne of grace I can receive mercy and rest in the finished work of Christ.

Experiencing Heaven Now

Precious believer, I pray you are gaining the understanding that we do not have to wait to *get to heaven* in order to *experience heaven.* So many believers are just "hanging on" until we can get there. Yet He desires to give us a good life, right now, while living here on earth. Remember, Jesus brought His world into ours.

It is time to ask God to invade your world completely by bringing His world into your life. Hebrews tells us that the Israelites could not enter into the land of rest because of their unbelief: "And to whom did God swear that they would never enter his rest if not to those who disobeyed? So we see that they were not able to enter, because of their unbelief" (Hebrews 3:18–19). The disobedience referred to is the Israelites' unwillingness to believe God. Their sin was unbelief. They never left Egypt in their hearts.

If we refuse the gift of grace, we have only legalism left. And the problem with legalism is that we cannot keep just a few choice laws; we must keep them all—an impossibility. The Law was holy; it was God's set of requirements so that He could dwell with His people. But all the while, the animal sacrifices that were required to cover sin were a type of sacrifice later to be made by Jesus on our behalf. Yes, He was the ultimate and final sacrifice. Now, each of us who believe is in right standing with the Father. And because of the righteousness of Christ, we also are righteous.

Again, Jesus did not just come to earth with a new set of rules. He came to point us to the Father and to teach us to carry the Word of God in our hearts. The key for demonstrating the Kingdom of God is all about renewing the mind, transforming our lives and having hearts sold out to God. Jesus came to give us life and life more abundantly. He is not a Lawgiver, but a Life giver. The New Testament states that the Law was given so that man would realize how much he needed a Savior. And, if you take a close look at the Law, you understand quickly how much we really do need a Savior. Thank God that we are no longer under the curse of the Law, and that we have been redeemed to experience the blessing.

Again, we read in Hebrews 4 that there is a place called *rest* in the finished work of Christ. In fact, *Jesus Himself is the Promised Land.* Yes, He is my promise, and when I am in Him, there is a continual outflow of milk and honey. What do I mean by that, and just what do the milk and honey represent? Well, they represent a land of plenty.

The word *milk* in Hebrew is derived from the word *cheleb* (pronounced *kheh*-leb), and it refers to "fatness, the best, richest or choice part." God has the richest land prepared for us, and when we are in Christ we dwell in the best, the choice part of life, the finest and richest life available.

And the word *honey* is from the Hebrew word *debash* (pronounced deb-*ash*), an unused root word meaning "gummy or sticky like syrup." Think about this for a second. God's very best is going to stick to us! Because of Christ's finished work at the cross, we can rest in the fact that He sticks closer than a brother; He will never leave us or forsake us. We can rest in the fact that His presence is always with us and that He has His very best planned for each of our lives.

Ambassadors on the Earth

Adam was God's ambassador to the earth. Whatever he named the animals became their names. The mandate to rule and reign on earth started with Adam in the Garden. The mandate for mankind has never changed; however, as you know, man lost his authority. Yet Christ was slain from the foundation of the world; and the Garden still speaks of the finished work of Christ.

Listen up again—we are headed somewhere important. Genesis 2 tells us that Adam was instructed to be a "garden-keeper." If you look throughout Scripture, you will notice a thread concerning the Garden and how the mandate to rule and reign was restored through Christ. In the New Testament, we read where Jesus prayed in a garden. His sweat was as drops of blood in a garden. He was arrested for the crucifixion in a garden. He was buried in a garden.

Why do you think a garden keeps coming up in this story? I believe that the mandate in the Garden of Eden was restored when Jesus was resurrected. We get, in a sense, a foreshadowing of this when Mary Magdalene saw Him after His resurrection—His first appearance—and thought He was the gardener. Well, He is! Read what Jesus said:

> I am the True Vine, and My Father is the Vinedresser. Any branch in Me that does not bear fruit [that stops bearing] He cuts away (trims off, takes away); and He cleanses and repeatedly prunes every branch that continues to bear fruit, to make it bear more and richer and more excellent fruit.
>
> You are cleansed and pruned already, because of the word which I have given you [the teachings I have discussed with you].
>
> Dwell in Me, and I will dwell in you. [Live in Me, and I will live in you.] Just as no branch can bear fruit of itself without abiding in (being vitally united to) the vine, neither can you bear fruit unless you abide in Me.
>
> I am the Vine; you are the branches. Whoever lives in Me and I in him bears much (abundant) fruit. However, apart from Me [cut off from vital union with Me] you can do nothing.
>
> John 15:1–5 AMPLIFIED

I love the promises given to us as long as we remain attached to Jesus. The Father is the Master Gardener. Jesus is a member of the Godhead and that makes Him a Gardener also. We have been put in the finished work of Christ, and we need only to guard and keep what Jesus has already accomplished. He wants to release heaven's power. He desires for us to be set free from all that limits us and become exporters of truth and light to others.

If you read about the Garden of Eden, you see that Scripture discusses the rivers that ran through it. Jesus is our River of Life, and He is restoring us as ambassadors on earth, ruling and reigning through His accomplished work at Calvary.

Adam was made in the image of God and was given power in the garden, as we previously discussed. Yet, as you know, he died. This was a shadow of a later garden-type dominion restored back to us through Christ.

The Promised Land

The promised land is *now*! It is *today*. There really is a "there"—a heaven; but we do not have to wait to go "there" to enjoy it. Yes, we can have heaven on earth today. This message is often lost. Too many embrace a doomsday mentality—even in the pulpit. But God is in the restoration business. His desire is to restore us, heal up the broken-hearted and demonstrate Kingdom power as never before.

God is declaring today to any pharaoh that attempts to rule over us: "Let My people go." We need to have faith that God desires to set all of His people free—all over the world. God's heart is for all to be saved and to know Him. The Lord said in Deuteronomy 30:11 that His command-ments to Israel were "not too difficult for you or beyond your reach." Looking again at the Old Testament and the Law with new lenses of grace, we realize that with His grace is the divine ability to remain obedient to all of His instructions and commands. Nothing is too difficult for us whenever we fully realize that we have His grace to empower us.

In the New Testament we are reminded of this passage. Basically, the Lord wants us to know that through Christ nothing is impossible. The Old Testament believers did not have the faith or the righteousness of Christ to defeat the enemy. We have the Living Word available to us every day.

> Brethren, my heart's desire and prayer to God for Israel is, that they might be saved. For I bear them record that they have a zeal of God, but not according to knowledge. For they being ignorant of God's righteousness, and going about to establish their own righteousness, have not submitted themselves unto the righteousness of God.
>
> For Christ is the end of the law for righteousness to every one that believeth. For Moses describeth the righteousness which is of the law, that the man which doeth those things shall live by them.
>
> But the righteousness which is of faith speaketh on this wise, Say not in thine heart, Who shall ascend into heaven? (that is, to bring Christ down from above:) or, Who shall descend into the deep? (that is, to bring up Christ again from the dead.)
>
> But what saith it? The word is nigh thee, even in thy mouth, and in thy heart: that is, the word of faith, which we preach; that if thou shalt confess with thy mouth the Lord Jesus, and shalt believe in thine heart that God hath raised him from the dead, thou shalt be saved.
>
> For with the heart man believeth unto righteousness; and with the mouth confession is made unto salvation.
>
> Romans 10:1–10 KJV

Let's not focus on what we should not believe. Let's end this book with something powerful to believe. Say this confession out loud:

*Jesus fulfilled the Law, and I am righteous. I believe in my
heart and confess His Word with my mouth. The Lord
Jesus Christ will bring the blessing to me and use me on
this earth to represent Him and His glory.*

The Arm of the Lord

Several years ago I had a dream about the arm of the Lord.
In the dream, I saw His arm stretched out to receive me,
and yet, at that same time, that same arm destroyed the
enemies who had been chasing me. I have never forgotten
that dream. It was so comforting to know that He was
destroying all of my adversaries. Let me ask you the same
question Isaiah asked: "Who hath believed our report?
And to whom is the arm of the LORD revealed?" (Isaiah
53:1 KJV, emphasis added).

Precious believer, He is revealing His mighty arm to you.

Maybe you have seen those World War II posters pictur-
ing women working in jobs traditionally held by men. They
are showing their strength and support of the war effort
by flexing their arm muscles. Picture it: God rolls up His
sleeves, then flexes His muscles! Remember, He wiped out
the Egyptians and said, "I did that with My arm and My
right hand." All of that power was with one hand. Even if
He had one hand tied behind His back, He could wipe out
thousands upon thousands upon thousands. Just imagine
what would happen if His whole body got involved. Wow!
That is my God. And you can also boldly say, *"Yes, that's
my God."*

I love the fact that each of us can experience *limitless
living.* By this I mean that there are absolutely no limits to

what we can do or experience with God on our side. This is why the title of this book is about *letting go*. When we let go of limitations, we can fully experience an unlimited lifestyle, which means that we are empowered to demonstrate His Kingdom. But it also means that we can experience freedom. Knowing this, we can do as Christ instructed and speak to any mountain—and it has to move (see Matthew 17:20). Jesus said that if we have faith even as small as a mustard seed then nothing will be impossible for us.

When we let go of doubt and unbelief, then, we are also taking the limits off of what we believe God will do for us. God is love, and I believe that He takes tremendous joy in blessing us. It is more than simply possessing *things*. It is all about experiencing the fullness of joy that comes with freedom. And when we know that we have freedom in Christ, and that we are hidden in Him, we can demonstrate His perfect will—and experience heaven on earth.

Jesus took every curse with Him to the cross. Everything I had coming to me under the Old Testament curse, Jesus took so that I could receive everything coming under the New Covenant promises. The Lord laid on Him the iniquity of us all. Yes, He took what *I* had coming so I could have what *He* had coming. Now we can enter into this promised land and rest in the finished work of Christ.

Only believe—and it is yours. Now that is a promise to end a book with!

Dr. Sandie Freed and her husband, Mickey, are the senior pastors of Lifegate Church International and are the founders and directors of Zion Ministries in Hurst, Texas.

Sandie is an ordained prophetess with Christian International Ministries and travels extensively teaching prophetic truths to the Body of Christ.

Sandie has written numerous books, including *Destiny Thieves: Defeat Seducing Spirits and Achieve Your Purpose in God*; *Conquering the Antichrist Spirit*; *Breaking the Threefold Demonic Cord*; and *Power in the Blood*. She is a featured guest on television and radio, where she shares her testimony of God's healing and delivering power. A gifted minister in dreams and visions and spiritual discernment, Sandie is a sought-after speaker and seminar instructor for her insight on dreams and visions and discerning demonic strongholds over individuals, churches and regions.

Sandie and Mickey have one daughter, Kimberly.

For more information, contact Sandie at

Zion Ministries
P.O. Box 54874
Hurst, TX 76054

Zionministries1@sbcglobal.net
www.sandiefreed.com
www.lifegatechurchinternational.com

More from Spiritual Warfare Expert Sandie Freed

To learn more about Sandie and her books, visit zionministries.us.

Three evil powers have joined forces to deceive you, rob you and imprison you in religious structures. It's time to fight back.

Breaking the Threefold Demonic Cord

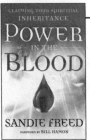

As a child of the King of kings, you have been born into a royal bloodline—and there is power in the blood! Awaken to your royal identity and claim the full inheritance that God has, through Jesus, already bestowed on you.

Power in the Blood

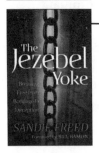

Break free from the spirits of deception, including Jezebel, in order to take hold of God's truth and receive your rightful blessings.

The Jezebel Yoke